McGraw-Hill/Contemporary's

Language Builder

Intermediate 2

McGraw-Hill Contemporary

Series Editor: Rebecca Grazulis
Executive Editor: Linda Kwil
Marketing Manager: Sean Klunder
Production Manager: Genevieve Kelley
Cover Designer: Michael E. Kelly

 **Wright Group**

ISBN 0-07-283588-5

Send all inquiries to:
Wright Group/McGraw-Hill
One Prudential Plaza
130 East Randolph Street, Suite 400
Chicago, IL 60601

Printed in the United States of America.

2 3 4 5 6 7 8 9 10 CUS 09 08 07 06 05

The *McGraw-Hill* Companies

◆ Contents

Contents *continued*

◆ To the Learner

If you have had problems expressing your ideas, particularly in writing, Contemporary's *Language Builder* will help. The workbook will explain basic grammar and composition skills and let you practice those skills in focused exercises. *Language Builder* will increase your confidence in your ability to communicate, both orally and in writing.

How does using Contemporary's *Language Builder* improve your language skills, particularly your writing skills? The workbook covers the following areas:

- grammar and usage
- sentence formation
- paragraph development
- capitalization
- punctuation
- writing conventions governing such special forms as letters and quotations

Included in the workbook are a Pretest and a Posttest. The Pretest will help you find your language strengths and weaknesses. Then you can use the workbook lessons to improve your skills. When you have finished the lessons and exercises, the Posttest will help you see if you have mastered those skills. Usually mastery means completing 80 percent of the questions correctly.

Language Builder will help you develop specific language skills, especially writing skills. The workbook is self-contained with the Answer Key at the back of the book. Clear directions will guide you through the lessons and exercises.

Each lesson in the workbook is divided into four parts:

 Introduce clearly defines, explains, and illustrates the skill. The examples prepare you for the work in the following exercises.

 Practice lets you work on the skill just introduced. If a skill requires additional explanation, this page (and, rarely, **Apply**) may add to the information presented in **Introduce.**

 Apply gives you a different way to practice the skill.

 Check Up provides a quick test on the skill covered in the lesson.

How to Use This Workbook

1. Take the Pretest on pages 7–14. Check your answers using the Answer Key on page 15. Refer to the Evaluation Chart on page 15 to find which skills you need to work on.

2. Take each four-page lesson one at a time. Ask your teacher for help with any problems you may have.

3. Use the Answer Key, which begins on page 207, to correct your answers after each exercise.

4. At the end of each unit, read the Unit Review and complete the Unit Assessment. These pages provide an opportunity to combine all the individual skills you have worked on and to check your progress on them. After you finish the Unit Assessment, your teacher may want to discuss your answers with you.

5. After you have finished all six units, take the Posttest on pages 198–205. Check your answers using the Answer Key on page 206. Then discuss your progress with your teacher.

◆ Pretest

Decide which punctuation mark, if any, is needed in each sentence.

1. After you examine the menu make your selection and stick to it.
   A ,   B .   C ?   D None

2. The electrician said that the job would take only one day
   F "   G .   H ,   J None

3. Jay, did you put bleach in the wash with Nanette's best blouse
   A ?   B !   C :   D None

4. "Ill be coming in late tomorrow," said the clerk.
   F "   G ,   H '   J None

5. Mrs. Wong needs a babysitter on these evenings Tuesday, Thursday, and Friday.
   A ,   B ;   C :   D None

Choose the word or phrase that best completes each sentence.

6. Terence worked _____ on this project than he ever worked before.

   F more hardly

   G hardly

   H harder

   J more harder

7. She is one of those performers _____ are never boring.

   A who

   B they

   C that

   D her

8. The cashier _____ on the new computers before the store opened.

   F train

   G will have trained

   H has trained

   J had trained

9. After the show, the singer happily signed _____ fans' programs.

   A hers

   B her

   C your

   D their

Read each set of sentences. Choose the sentence that is written correctly and has correct capitalization and punctuation.

10. F   Alex asked, "How will we celebrate New Year's Eve"?

    G   "Let's go dancing, Debbie said.

    H   "Today's paper," she continued, "Lists events all around town."

    J   The ad for the dinner-dance said that party hats were included.

11. A   Took pencils for granted.

    B   Where does the lead used in pencils come from?

    C   Before pencils were invented.

    D   People used quill pens they got the quills from birds.

12. F   After Marnie rearranged the furniture, the room looked larger.

    G   Nick called an interior designer next week.

    H   He had compared prices before he makes up his mind.

    J   As the adults talked, the children will fall asleep before the TV.

13. A   Both my Father and aunt Edna like crossword puzzles.

    B   Last july Edna bought a book of puzzles at mel's bookstore.

    C   The theme of one puzzle was National Parks in the United States.

    D   Some clues were photos of parks such as Mesa Verde in Colorado.

14. F   What time do you raise in the morning?

    G   The sound of some alarm clocks is loud enough to rise the dead.

    H   I set my alarm for 7:00 A.M.

    J   I also sit my clock far from my bed to force myself out of bed.

15. A   Every music lover has an opinion about their favorite composer.

    B   A conductor may have an opinion about an audience, and they're not always positive.

    C   People in one audience cleared their throats loudly.

    D   The conductor showed him irritation by stopping the music.

16. F   Can you tell me where to find the manager?

    G   Kindly repeat that again, please.

    H   The loud, blaring, ear-splitting music drowned out your voice.

    J   Because of the noise, I avoid this place and hardly ever come here.

17. A   Nathan said "I read a funny story about President Coolidge."

    B   "What could be funny," Lois asked, "about Silent Cal?"

    C   Nathan replied "that someone bragged the president would say more than two words to him."

    D   Coolidge said, "you lose".

Read each set of underlined sentences. Then choose the sentence that best combines the underlined sentences.

18. Karen bought a bottle of salad dressing.
    The dressing was fat-free.

    F Karen bought a bottle of fat-free salad dressing.

    G Karen bought a fat-free bottle of salad dressing.

    H Karen, who bought a bottle of salad dressing, bought a dressing that was fat-free.

    J Karen bought a bottle of salad dressing, but the dressing was fat-free.

19. Clouds drifted across the sky.
    The clouds were white.
    The sky was blue.

    A Clouds that drifted across the sky were white and blue.

    B White clouds drifted across the sky, which was blue.

    C Clouds that were white drifted across a sky that was blue.

    D White clouds drifted across the blue sky.

20. Frank packed some clothes in his suitcase.
    He packed his camera in his suitcase.
    He packed some film in his suitcase.

    F Frank packed some clothes and his camera in his suitcase, and he packed some film.

    G Frank packed some clothes, his camera, and some film in his suitcase.

    H Frank packed some clothes in his suitcase and his camera in his suitcase and some film in his suitcase.

    J Frank, in his suitcase, packed some clothes, and he packed his camera and film.

21. Margo set her watch forward one hour.
    She traveled to a different time zone.

    A Margo set her watch forward one hour, or she traveled to a different time zone.

    B Because Margo set her watch forward one hour, she traveled to a different time zone.

    C Because Margo traveled to a different time zone, she set her watch forward one hour.

    D One hour Margo set her watch forward, and it traveled to a different time zone.

Read each paragraph. Then choose the sentence that best fills the blank.

22. _____. From the time she was a baby gorilla, Koko was taught American Sign Language. She has proved her understanding of language in numerous ways. For example, at three years old, she expressed thirst and impatience by signing "Drink, hurry." When her mate Michael died, Koko signed such words as "sorry" and "cry." In happier moods, she tells jokes. One time she put a tube to her nose and signed "elephant."

F   Many pet owners claim that their pets can "speak" to them.

G   Koko is one remarkable gorilla.

H   American Sign Language has its own grammar rules.

J   Gorillas are probably more intelligent than any other animal.

23. Do you want to transplant a small tree? Your job begins in the fall of the year before the move. Dig a circle around the plant up to a foot deep to cut off distant roots. _____. The following spring, when you dig up the tree, follow the line of the same circle. That way you will not disturb the new, healthy roots.

A   During the following weeks, the tree will develop new roots close to the base.

B   If the tree is too big, call in a professional landscaper.

C   If necessary, soak the ground first to make digging in it easier.

D   Don't wait too long to begin the job.

24. Some words have interesting stories behind them. _____. An English nobleman liked playing cards better than doing anything else. He didn't even want to leave the card table to eat! He had his servants bring him meat and other foods placed between two slices of bread. Then he could eat at the card table without letting plates or silverware get in the way of the cards. Because the cardplayer was the Earl of Sandwich, his snack became known as a *sandwich*.

F   Nevertheless, consider the word *sandwich*.

G   On the other hand, consider the word *sandwich*.

H   For example, consider the word *sandwich*.

J   Similarly, consider the word *sandwich*.

25.   In Greek mythology, the hero Hercules was given twelve extremely difficult tasks. One task was to clean the stables of the king Augeas. The stables held so many horses that it was impossible for a single person to sweep out more than one small area at a time. _____. With his great strength, Hercules changed the route of two rivers. The rivers then flowed into the stables and cleared the floors.

   A Consequently, Hercules used a river instead of a broom.

   B In other words, Hercules used a river instead of a broom.

   C Primarily, Hercules used a river instead of a broom.

   D Afterward, Hercules used a river instead of a broom.

26.   When Barb goes to the farmers' market held in a downtown parking lot, she doesn't want to miss a single stall. _____. Then she walks east, looking only at stalls on her left. At the end of the row, she turns around and walks west, again looking only to her left. She repeats the process for each row. Finally, after seeing every stall, she reverses her route. This time she stops along the way to buy things.

   F Even if the cost at the market is higher than at the supermarket, the quality of the vegetables is almost always better.

   G She starts with the flower sellers in the northwest corner of the lot.

   H The market is held every Saturday from May through October.

   J She goes early in the morning to get the best produce.

Read each topic sentence. Then choose the answer that best develops the topic sentence.

27. Bill Veeck was one of the most entertaining team owners in major league baseball.

   A During his long career in baseball, Veeck owned three different major league teams: the Cleveland Indians, the St. Louis Browns, and the Chicago White Sox. He was elected to the Baseball Hall of Fame in 1991.

   B Bill Veeck was born February 9, 1914, in Chicago, Illinois. He died in Chicago on January 2, 1986. In 1962, he wrote an autobiography, *Veeck—As in Wreck.*

   C Veeck introduced the exploding scoreboard, used fireworks and contests to lure fans, and built exciting teams. His most famous stunt occurred in 1951. As owner of the St. Louis Browns, Veeck signed a midget to a contract and sent him into a game as a pinch hitter wearing a uniform with the number 1/8.

   D Long called America's "national pastime," baseball now faces strong competition from football, soccer, and other sports. Players' strikes, high ticket prices, and other problems are wearing away baseball's fan base.

28. Every community can, at relatively little cost, provide its residents with opportunities to recycle.

F Some household materials that should be recycled are aluminum cans, glass, and paper. The cans can be melted and reused in new cans; glass can be ground up and used in new jars and bottles. Paper and cardboard can be reused not only in paper but also in insulation and other products.

G Establishing drop-off centers where residents can easily leave paper, glass, aluminum cans, and other materials is one way to encourage recycling. To make recycling even easier, a community can operate curbside collection programs.

H Every community faces many demands for services, of which waste collection is only one. Citizens who want their communities to get involved in recycling often need to express their opinions over a long period before they get a favorable response.

J A waste-processing plant has such equipment as conveyor belts and magnets to separate solid materials. Liquids, such as used motor oil, can also be recycled.

Read each paragraph. Then choose the sentence that does <u>not</u> belong in the paragraph.

29.   **1.** In English, the names of the days come mostly from mythology. **2.** Tuesday, Wednesday, and Thursday honor Tiu, Woden, and Thor, all gods in German and Norse myths. **3.** Friday honors Frigg, a Norse goddess. **4.** Some of the names of months come from numbers and real people.

A Sentence 1	**C** Sentence 3
B Sentence 2	**D** Sentence 4

30.   **1.** Whenever Daylight Savings Time begins and ends, Leonard is confused. **2.** Most of the United States observes Daylight Savings Time. **3.** The slogan "Spring forward; fall back" helps Leonard somewhat. **4.** To be safe, however, he doesn't change his clocks till he hears a radio announcer state the time.

F Sentence 1	**H** Sentence 3
G Sentence 2	**J** Sentence 4

Read the letter and the paragraphs and look at the numbered, underlined parts. Choose the answer that is written correctly for each underlined part.

(31) <u>july 5 2004</u>

Colossal Productions

(32) <u>449 Hay Street</u>

(33) <u>Fayetteville North Carolina 28301</u>

(34) <u>Dear sir or madam,</u>

(35)   Last night I attended the <u>independence day concert</u> your company presented,

(36) but I never heard the music. The sound system at the concert was <u>more worser</u> than any I had ever heard before! When those of us in the balcony complained, we were told nothing could be done to improve the sound. Since I did not get what I paid for, I'm requesting a refund. I have enclosed a photocopy of my ticket.

(37) <u>My address and phone number</u> are also on the photocopy.

(38) <u>Your Dissatisfied Customer—</u>
Roger Karnes
Roger Karnes

31.
  A july 5, 2004
  B July, 5, 2004
  C July 5, 2004
  D Correct as it is

32.
  F 449 hay street,
  G 449 Hay street
  H 449, hay street
  J Correct as it is

33.
  A Fayetteville, North Carolina 28301
  B Fayetteville, North Carolina, 28301
  C Fayetteville North Carolina, 28301
  D Correct as it is

34.
  F Dear Sir or Madam;
  G Dear Sir or madam,
  H Dear Sir or Madam:
  J Correct as it is

35.
  A Independence day concert
  B Independence Day concert
  C Independence Day: concert
  D Correct as it is

36.
  F worser
  G worse
  H much badder
  J Correct as it is

37.
  A my address and phone number
  B My Address and Phone Number
  C My address, and phone number,
  D Correct as it is

38.
  F Your dissatisfied customer,
  G Your Dissatisfied Customer,
  H Your dissatisfied customer:
  J Correct as it is

(39)   The world's longest-running musical was an American <u>play *The Fantasticks*</u>.
(40)   For almost forty-two years it was presented in a small <u>off-broadway theater in</u>
<u>New york</u>. This musical was based on a play named *Les Romanesques,* or "The
(41)   Romancers," by the noted <u>French Writer Edmund Rostand</u>. It tells of a girl and a
boy more in love with love than with each other. At one point the girl, who wishes
(42)   to be special, <u>prays, "Dear God don't</u> let me be normal!"

39. **A** play, *The Fantasticks*

B play, *the Fantasticks*

C play; *The Fantasticks*

D Correct as it is

41. **A** french writer Edmund Rostand

B french writer, Edmund Rostand

C French writer, Edmund Rostand

D Correct as it is

40. **F** off-broadway theater in New York

G off-Broadway theater in New York

H off-Broadway Theater in New York

J Correct as it is

42. **F** prays "Dear God don't

G prays, "Dear God dont

H prays, "Dear God, don't

J Correct as it is

(43)   For many years, Geraldine's hobbies have been <u>collecting teacups and to</u>
(44)   <u>make</u> Christmas tree ornaments. She <u>will acquire</u> three dozen teacups in different
(45)   patterns even before she got her first apartment. Now her <u>collection of teacups fill</u>
(46)   <u>an entire display case</u> in her living room. The huge case <u>doesn't hardly leave any</u>
room for her other furniture.

43. **A** to collect teacups and to make

B to collect teacups and making

C collecting teacups and she makes

D Correct as it is

45. **A** collection of teacups fill an
entirely display case

B collection of teacups fills an entire
display case

C collection of teacups entirely fill a
display case

D Correct as it is

44. **F** was acquiring

G will have acquired

H had acquired

J Correct as it is

46. **F** does'nt hardly leave any

G leaves hardly any

H doesn't leave no

J Correct as it is

Pretest Answer Key and Evaluation Chart

This Evaluation Chart will help you find the language skills you need to study. Circle the questions you answered incorrectly and go to the practice pages covering those skills.

Key

1.	A	24.	H	
2.	G	25.	A	
3.	A	26.	G	
4.	H	27.	C	
5.	C	28.	G	
6.	H	29.	D	
7.	A	30.	G	
8.	J	31.	C	
9.	B	32.	J	
10.	J	33.	A	
11.	B	34.	H	
12.	F	35.	B	
13.	D	36.	G	
14.	H	37.	D	
15.	C	38.	F	
16.	F	39.	A	
17.	B	40.	G	
18.	F	41.	C	
19.	D	42.	H	
20.	G	43.	A	
21.	C	44.	H	
22.	G	45.	B	
23.	A	46.	G	

Tested Skills	Question Numbers	Practice Pages
pronouns	7, 9	22–25, 26–29
antecedent agreement	15	30–33
verbs	8, 12, 44	34–37, 38–41, 42–45
subject/verb agreement	45	46–49
easily confused verbs	14	50–53
adjectives and adverbs	6, 36	54–57, 58–61, 62–65
use of negatives	46	66–69
sentence recognition	11	74–77, 78–81
sentence combining	18, 19, 20, 21	82–85, 86–89, 90–93
sentence clarity	16, 43	94–97, 98–101, 102–105
topic sentences	22	110–113, 114–117
supporting sentences	27, 28	118–121
sequence	23, 26	122–125
unrelated sentences	29, 30	126–129
connectives and transitions	24, 25	130–133
proper nouns and proper adjectives	13, 35, 37, 40, 41	138–141, 142–145
end marks	2, 3	154–157
commas	1, 39, 42	158–161, 162–165, 166–169
semicolons and colons	5	170–173
quotations	10, 17	178–181
apostrophes in contractions and possessives	4	182–185, 186–189
letter parts	31, 32, 33, 34, 38	190–193

Correlation Chart

Correlations Between Contemporary's Instructional Materials and TABE™ Language

Language   **Pretest Score** _____   **Posttest Score** _____

Subskill	TABE™ Form 7	TABE™ Form 8	Practice and Instruction Pages			
			Language Builder Intermediate 2	*Pre-GED Language Arts, Writing*	*Complete Pre-GED*	*English Exercises (1–5)**
27 Usage						
pronouns	4, 51, 53	4, 35, 51	22–25, 26–29	30–40	46–47, 78–82	1: 19–21
antecedent agreement	14		30–33	41–44	82	1: 22 3: 9
verb tenses	6, 7, 38, 46	5, 9, 32, 48	34–37, 38–41, 42–45	51–66	48–49, 89–111	1: 12–18 3: 5–6
subject/verb agreement		38, 45	46–49	67–76	113–124	2: 8–18
easily confused verbs	17	14	50–53			
adjectives	49	6, 46	54–57	81–94	49–50, 127–129	1: 23, 25, 27–28
adverbs	26		58–61	81–94	51–52, 130–131	1: 23, 24, 27–28
choosing between adjectives/adverbs	5, 44, 54	31, 37	62–65	85–86, 91	132	
use of negatives	37, 45	54	66–69	91–92		1: 26
28 Sentence Formation						
sentence recognition	8, 10, 48	7, 34	74–77, 78–81	13–18	57–68	2: 3–7, 23–26 4: 9–10
sentence combining	21, 22, 23, 24	17, 18, 19, 20	82–85, 86–89, 90–93	101–110	139–148	2: 19–22
sentence clarity	12, 39, 55	10, 36, 43	94–97, 98– 101, 102–105	95–98, 111–120	159–163	3: 3–4, 10–11

* Numbers correspond to the following titles: 1 = *Mastering Parts of Speech;* 2 = *Using Correct Sentence Structure;* 3 = *Improving Writing Style and Paragraphing;* 4 = *Building Punctuation Skills;* 5 = *Improving Spelling and Capitalization*

Subskill	TABE™ Form 7	TABE™ Form 8	Practice and Instruction Pages			
			Language Builder Intermediate 2	*Pre-GED Language Arts, Writing*	*Complete Pre-GED*	*English Exercises (1–5)**
29 Paragraph Development						
topic sentences	25, 26	21, 22	110–113, 114–117	157–161	150–155	3: 15–16
supporting sentences	31, 32	27, 28	118–121		150–155	3: 27–28
sequence	28, 29	23, 25	122–125	165–169	150–155	3: 22
unrelated sentences	33, 34	29, 30	126–129	165–169	150–155	3: 17–18
connectives/ transitions	27, 30	24, 26	130–133		150–155	3: 19–20
30 Capitalization						
proper nouns and proper adjectives	11, 13, 16, 18	8, 11, 13, 16, 33	138–141, 142–145	23–24, 133–138	71–74	5: 18–20, 23
first words and titles of works	52		146–149	134	59	5: 17, 22, 25
31 Punctuation						
end marks	1, 35		154–157	19–21, 139–140	59	4: 3–4
commas	3, 9, 19, 50	2, 12, 15, 44, 49, 50, 55	158–161, 162–165, 166–169	141–144	142–143, 149, 166–169	4: 5–8, 11
semicolons		53	170–173	145	149	4: 12–13
32 Writing Conventions						
quotations	2, 15	1, 3, 39, 52	178–181	145–146	133–134	4: 22–25
apostrophes in contractions and possessive nouns	20, 47		182–185, 186–189	27–28, 146, 149–150	81, 83	4: 17–19
letter parts	40, 41, 42, 43	40, 41, 42, 47	190–193		105–107	5: 24

* Numbers correspond to the following titles: 1 = *Mastering Parts of Speech*; 2 = *Using Correct Sentence Structure*; 3 = *Improving Writing Style and Paragraphing*; 4 = *Building Punctuation Skills*; 5 = *Improving Spelling and Capitalization*

Corresponds to TABE™ Forms 7 and 8
Tests of Adult Basic Education are published by CTB Macmillan/McGraw-Hill. Such company has neither endorsed nor authorized this test preparation book.

Recognizing and Using Nouns

Everything in the world around us has a name. The name of a person, place, or thing is called a **noun.** We use nouns to name anything that can be sensed as well as ideas and feelings, such as *wisdom* and *happiness.*

> Filled with <u>anxiety</u>, the <u>explorer</u> slowly crawled into the <u>cave</u>.

In the example above, all the nouns are singular. That is, they name only one person, place, thing, or idea. Nouns can also be plural; that is, they can name more than one of anything. Usually, plural nouns end in *s*.

> The <u>explorer</u> saw <u>bats</u> on the <u>ceiling</u> and <u>spiders</u> on the <u>floor</u>.
>   singular   plural   singular   plural   singular

However, the plurals of some nouns are formed in unusual ways. Plural forms like the following must be memorized:

man—men	woman—women	child—children
mouse—mice	foot—feet	tooth—teeth

Nouns can be common or proper. A **common noun** is the general name of any person, place, or thing.

> When going into the <u>cave</u>, the <u>explorer</u> carried several <u>flashlights</u>.

A **proper noun** is the name of a particular person, place, or thing. Begin each important word in a proper noun with a capital letter.

> <u>Lucia</u> will visit <u>Mammoth Cave National Park</u> in <u>Kentucky</u>.

Underline the singular nouns in each sentence. Circle the plural nouns. Remember that some proper nouns may have more than one word.

1. The children drew pictures on the sidewalk.

2. Pioneers crossed the Great Plains in covered wagons.

3. Miller's Department Store is having a sale on sheets and blankets.

4. Candice pointed out the stars of the Big Dipper.

5. The camels crossed the Sahara Desert with its huge sand dunes.

6. Leonardo da Vinci painted the famous portrait named *Mona Lisa*.

7. Trees in our neighborhood lost branches during the thunderstorm.

8. When Andrew graduated, Mrs. Hoffman was filled with pride.

B Practice

On the line beside each common noun, write a matching proper noun. For example, to match the common noun *author*, you might use the proper noun *Mark Twain*.

1. athlete _____

2. country _____

3. building _____

4. document _____

5. entertainer _____

6. month _____

7. city _____

8. school _____

9. street _____

10. actor _____

Write a noun on each line to complete each sentence. The kind of noun that is needed is described in parentheses ( ).

11. After the emcee introduced _____ (proper), the crowd cheered.

12. Bringing _____ (plural) onto public transportation is forbidden.

13. The _____ (singular) has not been working properly for days.

14. When I have to speak to a large audience, I am filled with _____ (common).

15. Tara turned her purse over and out fell _____ (plural).

16. Someday I would like to visit _____ (proper).

17. Marie rode to the airport in a _____ (singular).

18. To get on this ride, _____ (plural) must be at least four feet tall.

19. The astronauts reported seeing _____ (common) from their spaceship.

20. The lawyer, _____ (proper), energetically defended her client.

C Apply

If the nouns in each sentence are not capitalized properly, rewrite the sentence correctly on the line. If the nouns are capitalized correctly, write *Correct* on the line.

1. The Olympic Games are held every four Years.

   _____

2. How much does the Westlake children's Zoo charge for Admission?

   _____

3. Many people enjoy high school football as much as professional football.

   _____

4. Marian anderson served the United states as a delegate to the united Nations.

   _____

5. President john F. kennedy took office in 1961.

   _____

6. hawaii is located in the pacific ocean.

   _____

7. Have you ever seen the Empire State Building in New York City?

   _____

For each item, write a sentence using the kinds of nouns described.

8. one proper noun and one common noun

   _____

9. one singular common noun and one plural common noun

   _____

10. one singular common noun and one singular proper noun

    _____

11. one proper noun, one singular common noun, and one plural common noun

    _____

D Check Up

Choose the phrase that describes the underlined word in each sentence.

1. The constellation <u>Orion</u> was visible in the southern sky.

   A plural common noun

   B singular proper noun

   C plural common noun

   D None of these

2. <u>Students</u> who took the test said it was fair but difficult.

   F plural proper noun

   G singular common noun

   H plural common noun

   J None of these

3. My car's <u>transmission</u> needs repair.

   A singular common noun

   B singular proper noun

   C plural common noun

   D None of these

4. The children <u>sat</u> watching the puppets for twenty minutes.

   F singular common noun

   G singular proper noun

   H plural common noun

   J None of these

5. When the ferry arrived, at least fifteen cars drove onto the <u>island</u>.

   A singular common noun

   B singular proper noun

   C plural common noun

   D None of these

6. Who was the architect who designed the <u>Guggenheim Museum</u>?

   F singular common noun

   G plural common noun

   H singular proper noun

   J None of these

7. When the whistle blew, the <u>workers</u> knew it was time to go home.

   A singular proper noun

   B plural proper noun

   C plural common noun

   D None of these

8. Julia is saving money to get her <u>teeth</u> straightened.

   F singular common noun

   G singular proper noun

   H plural common noun

   J None of these

9. The bus broke down in the <u>Rocky Mountains</u>.

   A plural common noun

   B plural proper noun

   C singular common noun

   D None of these

10. <u>Although</u> the whole day was cloudy, the rain held off until after midnight.

    F singular common noun

    G singular proper noun

    H plural proper noun

    J None of these

Personal Pronouns

Tina forgot Tina's list when Tina went to the grocery store.

The repetition of Tina's name in this sentence is awkward.
Using pronouns in place of her name improves the sentence.

Tina forgot <u>her</u> list when <u>she</u> went to the grocery store.

Her and *she* refer to Tina. These words are examples of pronouns.
Pronouns are words used in place of nouns. One kind of pronoun,
the **personal pronoun**, is used in place of a person's name. A
personal pronoun can also refer to a thing.

Tina got the last <u>cart</u>. <u>It</u> had a squeaky wheel. (*It* refers to *cart*.)

Pronouns are classified by number, gender, and person.

Number: Pronouns that refer to one thing are singular. Pronouns that refer to more
than one thing are plural.

Gender: Pronouns that refer to males are masculine (*he, him, his*). Pronouns that refer
to females are feminine (*she, her, hers*). Pronouns that refer to things or
animals are neuter (*it, its*).

Person: Some pronouns refer to the person who is speaking. These are called first-
person pronouns. Other pronouns, called second-person pronouns, refer to
the person who is spoken to. Third-person pronouns refer to other people,
places, or things.

	<u>Singular</u>	<u>Plural</u>
First Person:	I, me, my, mine	we, us, our, ours
Second Person:	you, your, yours	you, your, yours
Third Person:	he, she, him, her, it, his, hers, its	they, them, their, theirs

Underline the personal pronoun in each sentence. Circle the noun it refers to.

1. Alex checked the equipment one last time, and then he set off for the mountaintop.

2. Phil, will you water the flowers by the front door?

3. The lawyers presented their final arguments to the jury.

4. After Kirsten makes only 350 more payments, the house belongs to her.

5. The citizens want good schools, but they are not always willing to pay more taxes.

6. Maria believes that she will win the lottery someday.

B Practice

Personal pronouns can be used as subjects of sentences, as objects, or to show possession. For each use, there are special forms.

Use the following pronouns as **subjects** in sentences or clauses:

> I   we   you   he, she, it   they

> Whenever <u>we</u> go to a Mexican restaurant, <u>I</u> always order burritos.

Use the following pronouns as **objects** of verbs or prepositions:

> me   us   you   him, her, it   them

> The waitress served <u>me</u> before she served <u>them</u>. (each pronoun used as object of verb *served*)
> She brought the food to <u>us</u> quickly. (object of preposition *to*)

Often, a pronoun is part of a compound subject or a compound object.

> Grace and <u>I</u> love the tacos at this restaurant.
> The hostess always seats Grace and <u>me</u> next to the window.

You may write a sentence with compound construction and become confused about which pronoun form to use. It may help to drop the noun that is used with the pronoun and say the sentence using the pronoun only. Your ear may tell you which is the correct form.

> ~~(Grace and)~~ I love the tacos at this restaurant.
> The hostess always seats ~~(Grace and)~~ me next to the window.

For each item, choose the sentence that is written correctly.

1. **A** The librarian read them a story about a talking dog.
   B The librarian read they a story about a talking dog.

2. **A** The secretaries and we will be attending a workshop.
   B The secretaries and us will be attending a workshop.

3. **A** Please repeat the instructions for Mr. Farrelli and I.
   B Please repeat the instructions for Mr. Farrelli and me.

4. **A** Dad and me are going to the ballpark tonight.
   B Dad and I are going to the ballpark tonight.

5. **A** We three sisters all share one bedroom.
   B Us three sisters all share one bedroom.

C ▶ Apply

Some personal pronouns show ownership or possession. They are called **possessive pronouns.** Unlike possessive nouns that use apostrophes to indicate ownership, possessive pronouns do not use apostrophes.

The chefs in the competition took great care with <u>their</u> special desserts. (*Their* refers to the noun *chefs*.)

	Singular Possessive	**Plural Possessive**
First Person:	my, mine	our, ours
Second Person:	your, yours	your, yours
Third Person:	his, her, hers, its	their, theirs

Most possessive pronouns have two forms. One form is used with a noun (*my* home; *our* home; *your, her, its, their* friends). The other form is used by itself (*mine, ours, yours, hers, theirs*).

The choice is <u>yours</u>. This is <u>your</u> choice.

Since pronouns take the place of nouns, they should match the nouns they replace in number, gender, and person.

The queen called for <u>her</u> ladies-in-waiting. (Both *queen* and *her* are singular, feminine, and third person.)

Underline the possessive pronoun in each sentence. Circle the word it refers to.

1. Grandfather is assembling photos of all his grandchildren.

2. Michelle has knitted scarves for her relatives.

3. The squirrels woke me up this morning with their loud chattering.

4. The students and their teachers are going on a field trip to the museum.

5. I shivered when the mountain cast its long shadow across the field.

Underline the possessive pronoun that correctly completes each sentence.

6. I would like you to meet (my, mine) sister.

7. If that car is (your, yours), would you please move it?

8. The responsibility is (her, hers) alone.

9. Is that (yours, your) final offer?

10. Eileen and Ted have bought a new table for (they're, their) apartment.

D ▸ Check Up

Choose the word or phrase that best completes each sentence.

1. The judge deliberated for an hour and then gave _____ verdict.

    A she

    B her

    C he

    D hers

2. The magician told _____ the secret to his famous trick.

    F she

    G his

    H me

    J I

3. Julio and _____ are headed downtown to see a movie.

    A I

    B him

    C me

    D my

4. We need a confirmation number for _____ files.

    F us

    G our

    H our's

    J ours

5. The reporter took pictures of Roy and _____ for the late edition.

    A we

    B his

    C they

    D them

6. For too long, the elephant was hunted for _____ valuable tusks.

    F its

    G it's

    H it

    J they

Each sentence has one word underlined. Choose the answer that is written correctly for the underlined word.

7. Minutes after Angela got home from work, <u>she</u> and Brian left again.

    A her

    B hers

    C them

    D Correct as it is

8. I am not sure where <u>them</u> were going in such a hurry.

    F they

    G their

    H their's

    J Correct as it is

Other Kinds of Pronouns

There are several other kinds of pronouns besides personal pronouns. The **demonstrative pronouns**—*this, that, these,* and *those*—point out particular persons, places, or things. *This* and *that* are singular; *these* and *those* are plural. Demonstrative pronouns may be used alone, or they may modify nouns. (The pronoun *them* is not a demonstrative pronoun.)

> Owen planted <u>this</u> tree. <u>This</u> is Owen's tree.
> <u>Those</u> shoes are muddy. <u>Those</u> are muddy shoes.

A **relative pronoun** introduces a relative clause. A relative clause is a group of words with a subject and a predicate that refers back to a noun or pronoun in the main part of the sentence. Unlike a complete sentence, the relative clause cannot stand on its own. Relative pronouns include the following: *who, whom, whose, which,* and *that.* Use *who* as the subject of a clause and *whom* as the object. Use *who* and *whom* to refer to people. Use *that* and *which* to refer to a thing, not a person.

> The admirer <u>who</u> sent the flowers included a card. (*who* refers to *admirer*)
> The dog <u>that</u> won first place was a collie. (*that* refers to *dog*)

Underline the demonstrative pronoun in each sentence.

1. Are these sweaters on sale today?

2. Who wrote the words to that song?

3. That was an exception to the rule.

4. This résumé seems most impressive to the boss.

5. You shouldn't eat fatty foods, so stay away from those doughnuts.

Circle the relative pronoun in each sentence. Draw an arrow from the relative pronoun to the noun or pronoun it refers to.

6. The hero to whom the medal was given accepted it shyly.

7. The mansion that was pictured in the magazine is open to the public.

8. Whisper the secret password to a woman who has a red rose on her lapel.

9. I once visited the country from which this stamp came.

10. The company, which had been in business for a century, recently went bankrupt.

B Practice

Reflexive pronouns end with -self (singular) or with -selves (plural).

	Singular	**Plural**
First person:	myself	ourselves
Second person:	yourself	yourselves
Third person:	himself, herself, itself	themselves

A reflexive pronoun reflects an action to a noun or pronoun used earlier in the sentence.

You should dress <u>yourself</u> in layers if you are going hiking.
Will Kim <u>himself</u> carry the backpack up the mountain?

Indefinite pronouns refer to people, places, and things in a general way, not to specific persons, places, or things. Some indefinite pronouns are always singular, some are always plural, and a few can be either singular or plural, depending on their use. If the pronoun refers to a single quantity, as in <u>all</u> of the book, it is singular. If it refers to plural items, as in <u>all</u> of the words, it is plural.

Singular	Plural	Either Singular or Plural
anybody, anyone, anything, each, either, everybody, everyone, everything, much, neither, nobody, no one, nothing, one, somebody, someone, something	both, few, many, several	all, more, most, none, some

Underline the reflexive and indefinite pronouns in each sentence. On the line write *REF* for reflexive or *IND* for indefinite.

1. _____ Kim made herself a pot of hot, strong coffee this morning.

2. _____ Will everyone in the department get a raise?

3. _____ Al woke himself up when he snored too loudly.

4. _____ The generals themselves gave the order to retreat.

5. _____ Some of the excitement died down after the bride and groom left.

6. _____ Most of the people who saw the movie liked it.

7. _____ All of the ketchup leaked out of the cracked bottle.

8. _____ Bob and Jane bought themselves a plasma TV.

C Apply

Write the type of pronoun described in parentheses to complete each sentence.

1. (demonstrative) Ask the movers to take _____ dishes into the kitchen.

2. (reflexive) The king _____ attended the ceremony.

3. (indefinite) _____ of the heat is going to the upstairs bedrooms.

4. (reflexive) The proud student gave _____ an A for his report.

5. (relative) I am tired of salespeople _____ call at dinnertime.

6. (demonstrative) _____ is the title of our book club's next selection.

7. (demonstrative) _____ is the folder that we thought was missing.

8. (reflexive) The woman wanted to give _____ a pedicure.

9. (indefinite) _____ of the desserts look delicious.

10. (relative) Did you hear the speech _____ the president gave?

Follow the instructions for each item.

11. Write a sentence using the indefinite pronoun *somebody*.

    _____

12. Write a sentence using the relative pronoun *who*.

    _____

13. Write a sentence using the demonstrative pronoun *this*.

    _____

14. Write a sentence using the reflexive pronoun *themselves*.

    _____

15. Write a sentence using the reflexive pronoun *myself*.

    _____

16. Write a sentence using the indefinite pronoun *all*.

    _____

D Check Up

Choose the pronoun in each sentence.

1. Several of the judges gave the diver a perfect score.

   A Several

   B judges

   C gave

   D perfect

2. The sound system in this theater is excellent.

   F system

   G this

   H theater

   J is

3. Barry himself chose the winning numbers.

   A Barry

   B himself

   C chose

   D winning

4. Pauline is shopping for a chair that is comfortable and attractive.

   F shopping

   G chair

   H that

   J comfortable

Choose the word that best completes each sentence.

5. Tell me what you would do in _____ situation.

   A these

   B those

   C this

   D which

6. We _____ were surprised when our team won the championship.

   F themself

   G himself

   H ourselves

   J ourselfs

7. Here is my partner, with _____ I worked on this project.

   A who

   B whose

   C whom

   D that

8. When _____ teams take the field, anything can happen.

   F this

   G these

   H what

   J that

A Introduce

Making Pronouns Agree with Their Antecedents

A **pronoun** is a word used in place of a noun. The word the pronoun replaces is called its **antecedent.** The antecedent usually comes before the pronoun in the same sentence or in a previous sentence.

> Regina is meeting <u>her</u> friends for lunch.
> (The antecedent of the pronoun *her* is *Regina*.)

Pronouns must agree with their antecedents in three ways. First, they must agree in number.

If the antecedent is singular, the pronoun must be singular. If the antecedent is plural, the pronoun must be plural. Antecedents that are nouns or pronouns joined by *and* are considered to be plural. Pay special attention to pronouns whose antecedents are indefinite pronouns. If you have questions about whether the indefinite pronoun is singular or plural, refer to the chart on page 27.

> *Justin* is painting <u>his</u> house gray. (singular)
> The *neighbors* painted <u>their</u> house last year. (plural)
> *Joe and Tom* have loaned Justin <u>their</u> ladder. (plural)
>
> *Neither* of the helpers brought <u>his</u> or <u>her</u> paintbrush. (singular)
> *Both* of the brothers are known for helping <u>their</u> friends. (plural)

Underline the pronoun in each sentence. Circle its antecedent.

1. Caitlin is making new curtains for her bedroom.

2. Several of the travelers lost their luggage.

3. When the concert was canceled, the fans demanded that they get refunds.

4. Dr. Frankenstein was shocked by the power of his creation.

5. The dog looked around the room for its favorite toy.

6. During the storm, everyone turned his or her windshield wipers on.

7. The storm did its damage between midnight and one o'clock.

8. Joan and Rita are planning a surprise party for their parents.

9. The hyena and the gazelle are known for their incredible speed.

10. Most of the students helped themselves to the handouts the speaker supplied.

B Practice

Secondly, pronouns must agree with their antecedents in gender. *He, him,* and *his* must have masculine antecedents. *She, her,* and *hers* must have feminine antecedents. *It* and *its* must have neuter antecedents. When the gender of an antecedent is unclear, as in a singular indefinite pronoun such as *everyone,* use phrases such as *he or she* and *his or her.*

> *Dave* picks up <u>his</u> son at day care every day. (masculine)
> *Sharon* left <u>her</u> car at the train station. (feminine)
> The *mosquito* bothered me when <u>it</u> flew around my ear. (neuter)
> *Everyone* was sure <u>his or her</u> choice was best. (singular indefinite)

Finally, pronouns must agree with their antecedents in person. Whether the antecedent is in the first person, second person, or third person, the pronoun should match it.

> *We* gave <u>ourselves</u> plenty of time to reach the airport. (first person)
> *You* <u>yourself</u> should visit Europe someday. (second person)
> The *inventor* had the idea, but <u>he</u> didn't get rich. (third person)

Remember that relative pronouns must agree with their antecedents. When the antecedents are people, use *who* and *whom.* When the antecedents are not people, use *which* and *that.*

> *Passengers* <u>who</u> come late must reschedule their flights.
> The *plane* <u>that</u> we took was nearly empty.

Underline the pronoun that completes each sentence correctly. Circle its antecedent.

1. Although the model was also a scientist, (you, she) kept her scientific work a secret.

2. The college thanked the millionaire (which, who) had contributed so much.

3. Everyone wants to know (his or her, their) score on the driving test right away.

4. Many of the students pass the test on (his or her, their) first try.

5. Swimmers can leave (his, their) belongings in the locker room.

6. The workers (themselves, ourselves) were running the company.

7. Amy and Lindsey signed (her, their) names on the petition.

8. Somebody left (his or her, their) lunch in the refrigerator for weeks.

9. The sweater (whom, that) I bought last week shrank in the dryer.

10. Brian was driving the car when (they, it) caught on fire.

Apply

Look for a pronoun-antecedent error in each sentence. If you find an error, rewrite the sentence correctly on the line. If there is no error, write *Correct* on the line.

1. The teacher that took a special interest in me was Mr. Wesley.

   _____

2. Anna Moses took up painting when he was more than 70 years old.

   _____

3. Both Dean and Paul hardly ever answer his phones on the first ring.

   _____

4. The guests hung their coats in the hall closet.

   _____

5. Most of the participants felt that his or her time was well spent.

   _____

6. The music hall, who was built in 1898, is being renovated.

   _____

7. Anybody with a password can access their account.

   _____

8. When Ellen and Megan met again, she screamed and hugged.

   _____

9. I washed this window twice because they still seemed dirty.

   _____

10. When Terri gets up too early, you get tired around three o'clock.

    _____

11. Either Sean, the plumber, or Ralph, the carpenter, left his tools here.

    _____

12. Many of the audience members got to our feet and applauded.

    _____

D Check Up

Choose the pronoun that completes each sentence correctly.

1. The players took _____ places in the field.

   A our

   B her

   C their

   D its

2. Dad _____ fixed the broken window.

   F yourself

   G ourselves

   H themselves

   J himself

3. The actress won praise for _____ work in the play.

   A his

   B her

   C ours

   D their

4. My friend, _____ used to be afraid of dogs, just got a Doberman.

   F who

   G whose

   H that

   J which

Choose the sentence that is written correctly.

5. A Lupe and Anna parked her cars in the garage.

   B We invited Sam and Barb, but they couldn't come.

   C Maybe Tim and Mark will bring his vacation pictures.

   D I might fire Ann and Kate, or I might give her a second chance.

6. F Neither of the umpires wore their face mask.

   G Both of the mothers took their toddlers to the playground.

   H Several of the boats had drifted away from its moorings.

   J One of the trees had lost all their leaves already.

7. A The directors gave themselves big raises.

   B Isaac excused ourselves and went to answer the phone.

   C We myself haven't read the book.

   D You yourselfs can repair the damage.

8. F Virginia is the artist which illustrated the children's book.

   G The car who led the parade was an old Model T.

   H A few of the people whom we invited brought gifts.

   J Do you know the lifeguard that is on duty today?

Verbs

Words that name actions or states of being are called **verbs.** Every complete sentence must have at least one verb. The verb may have more than one word; such a phrase is called a **verb phrase.**

> Lee <u>was painting</u> near the mountains. The scenery there <u>is</u> spectacular.

Verbs that show state of being, such as *is*, never have objects. However, some of them link the subject of a sentence with another noun, a pronoun, or an adjective. These verbs are called **linking verbs.**

> Lee <u>is</u> a painter. (*Is* links *Lee* and *painter*.)
> Lee <u>is</u> talented. (*Is* links *Lee* and *talented*.)
> Lee <u>is</u> near the mountains. (no link)

A few verbs are used as **helping verbs** with other verbs. Helping verbs such as *can, must, will, shall, would,* and *should* are used before the base form of another verb.

> You <u>*should* see</u> Lee's portraits of his friends.

Underline the verbs and verb phrases in each of the following sentences.

1. After Diane complained to her councilman, a city crew repaired the park benches.

2. The baby's temperature is high.

3. When you arrive at the top of the mountain, plant this flag there.

4. Many new customers have come to the sale because the prices are unusually low.

5. Local weather forecasts predicted storms for today, but no rain has fallen yet.

6. Detroit has been a center of the auto industry for almost a century.

7. Although the restaurant was busy, we got a table quickly.

8. Is the soup still too hot?

9. John planted tomatoes and cucumbers this spring.

10. The old apple tree fell over during the thunderstorm.

11. The Larsons are our new neighbors.

12. You should see Genevieve's new puppy.

Every verb has **principal parts.** The following chart names the parts and gives examples of them.

Present Tense	Past Tense	Past Participle
train	trained	(has) trained
study	studied	(has) studied
fall	fell	(has) fallen
go	went	(has) gone

A verb is a **regular verb** if its past tense and past participle are both formed by adding *-ed* or *-d* to the present tense form. The verbs *train* and *study* in the chart above are examples of regular verbs. A verb is an **irregular verb** if its principal parts do not follow that pattern. Both *fall* and *go* are irregular verbs.

The irregular verbs *be, do,* and *have* are particularly important because they are used both as main verbs and helping verbs. The following chart lists their principal parts that form in irregular ways.

Present Tense	Past Tense	Past Participle
be	was, were	(has) been
do	did	(has) done
have	had	(has) had

Examine the verbs in the following chart. In the fourth column of the chart, write *R* after each of the regular verbs and *I* after each of the irregular verbs.

Present Tense	Past Tense	Past Participle	
break	broke	(has) broken	
carry	carried	(has) carried	
drink	drank	(has) drunk	
feed	fed	(has) fed	
freeze	froze	(has) frozen	
move	moved	(has) moved	
sing	sang	(has) sung	
steal	stole	(has) stolen	
swim	swam	(has) swum	
teach	taught	(has) taught	

C Apply

Transitive verbs, that is, verbs that pass action on to a person or thing, can be divided into two groups. They can be either active or passive. A verb is in **active voice** when the person or thing that performs the action is named before the verb, and the thing that receives the action is named after it.

> The weather bureau <u>has predicted</u> a foot of snow. (The weather bureau is <u>doing</u> the predicting.)

A verb is in **passive voice** when the person or thing that receives the action is named before the verb. The person or thing that performs the action may be named at the end of the sentence after *by.*

> A foot of snow <u>has been predicted</u> by the weather bureau. (The foot of snow is <u>receiving</u> the action. The weather bureau is <u>doing</u> the action.)

Every passive verb includes a helping verb that is a form of *be.*

> Many children *<u>are excited</u>* by the forecast.
> Unfortunate drivers *<u>will be</u>* <u>trapped</u> in slow-moving traffic.

On the line after each sentence, write *A* if the underlined verb is in active voice or *P* if it is in passive voice.

1. These plants are watered twice a week. _____

2. My husband and I are buying a new car. _____

3. My favorite show was canceled by the network. _____

4. Fewer butterflies have been sighted this year than in previous years. _____

5. Players have been signing autographs for over half an hour. _____

6. Classical music is broadcast by a rather small number of stations. _____

Follow the instructions for each of the following items.

7. Using active voice, write a sentence with the verb *brought.*

   _____

8. Using passive voice, write a sentence with the verb *are worn.*

   _____

9. Using active voice, write a sentence with the verb *will cut.*

   _____

D Check Up

Choose the verb or verb phrase that best completes each sentence.

1. During the 1500s, adventurers from many European countries _____ the world.

   A are explored

   B are explore

   C exploring

   D explored

2. Our firm _____ to use recycled paper.

   F is preferred

   G prefers

   H has prefer

   J preferring

3. To get a driver's license, teens _____ driver's ed.

   A must took

   B must take

   C must taking

   D must taken

4. The rising flood waters _____ houses on this street by tomorrow morning.

   F did damaged

   G damaging

   H will damage

   J will damaged

For each item, choose the sentence that is written correctly.

5. A Last week, the doctor gave Rod a new prescription.

   B Last week, the doctor giving Rod a new prescription.

   C Last week, the doctor given Rod a new prescription.

   D Last week, the doctor was given to Rod a new prescription.

6. F Ms. Wagner being the new owner of the house on the corner.

   G Ms. Wagner be the new owner of the house on the corner.

   H Ms. Wagner is the new owner of the house on the corner.

   J Ms. Wagner is been the new owner of the house on the corner.

7. A Construction on the new mall been stopped.

   B Construction on the new mall has stopping.

   C Construction on the new mall has stop.

   D Construction on the new mall has stopped.

8. F Submarines were using in warfare as early as the Civil War.

   G Submarines used in warfare as early as the Civil War.

   H Submarines have used in warfare as early as the Civil War.

   J Submarines were used in warfare as early as the Civil War.

Verbs and Their Tenses

A verb changes its form to indicate the time of its action. A verb's different forms are its **tenses.** The present, past, and future tenses are called the **simple tenses.**

> **Present:** Little Molly <u>watches</u> the TV. She and I <u>watch</u> together.
> **Past:** Yesterday afternoon she <u>watched</u> a program for children.
> **Future:** Tomorrow we <u>will watch</u> a cartoon show.

The **present tense** is used to indicate an action that happens now or on a regular basis.

> We <u>watch</u> TV every day.
> Molly's favorite show <u>starts</u> at 3:00 this afternoon.

For most verbs, the present tense forms follow the pattern shown below for *talk*. The forms of *have* and *be* are different.

> **talk:** I talk, you talk, she talks, we talk, they talk
>
> **has:** I have, you have, he has, we have, they have
>
> **be:** I am, you are, it is, we are, they are

The **past tense** is used to indicate an action that happened in the past. For any regular verb, the past tense is formed by adding *-ed* or *-d* to the present tense form. Irregular verbs form their past tense in many different ways. If you are unsure of the past tense of an irregular verb, look up the verb in a dictionary. The verb *be* has two past tense forms: *was* (singular) and *were* (plural).

The **future tense** is used to indicate an action that has not yet happened but will occur in the future. The future tense is formed by using a helping verb such as *will* or *shall* with the present tense form.

For each sentence, underline the verb or verb phrase that matches the tense listed.

1. *Present:* Squirrels (hid, hide, will hide) acorns in the lawn.

2. *Past:* The teller (asked, asks, will ask) George for identification.

3. *Present:* Nobody else (will have, had, has) the key for this lock.

4. *Future:* I (pick, will pick, picked) you up on my way home from work.

5. *Present:* Probably you (knew, know, will know) the answer to this question.

6. *Past:* The British troops (expected, expect, will expect) the colonial soldiers to flee.

7. *Future:* The store (notifies, notified, will notify) you when the picture frame arrives.

B Practice

The **progressive tenses** indicate actions that continue for some time. Each progressive tense is formed by combining a form of *be* with the present tense form of the main verb and *-ing*. To form the simple progressive tenses, use these forms of *be* with the main verb: present progressive—*am, is, are*; past progressive—*was, were*; future progressive—*will be*.

Aldo <u>is learning</u> how to ski. (present progressive)

Last week he <u>was falling</u> on every slope. (past progressive)

Soon, however, he <u>will be gliding</u> smoothly over the snow. (future progressive)

Choose the verb or verb phrase that correctly completes the sentence.

1. In 1492, Columbus's crew _____ for months without sight of land.

   A will be sailing

   B will sailing

   C was sailing

   D was sailed

2. Over the next few months, the company _____ sales of the newest toys.

   F will be tracking

   G tracks

   H will tracking

   J was track

3. Don't call before 7:00 because we _____ dinner until then.

   A were eating

   B will eating

   C eating

   D will be eating

4. Right now, Adelle _____ tomatoes in her garden.

   F was picking

   G is picking

   H will be picking

   J picked

5. None of us paid attention to the time while we _____ down the river.

   A will be floating

   B are floating

   C were floating

   D float

6. The jade plant _____ too big for the container it is in.

   F were growing

   G growing

   H was growing

   J is growing

 **Apply**

Verbs that describe actions occurring at about the same time should be consistent. That is, when you talk or write about two actions that happen at about the same time, you should use verbs that are in the same tense—present, past, or future.

If both actions happen for a limited time, use the same simple tense for both.

> **Example:** When the tree <u>fell</u>, everyone <u>heard</u> the crash. (both past)

If both actions continue for some time, use the same progressive tense for both.

> **Example:** As the tree <u>was falling</u>, a movie camera <u>was recording</u> the event. (both past progressive)

If one action continues and the other does not, use a progressive tense and a simple tense.

> **Example:** People <u>were walking</u> down a nearby path when the tree <u>fell</u>. (past progressive and past)

Underline the verb form that best completes each sentence.

1. While the search party was looking in the water for the lost boy, he (is sleeping, was sleeping, slept) on the beach.

2. Edgar pressed the doorbell until someone (answers, answered, was answering) the door.

3. Whenever I (worked, am working, will be working) in the backyard, the phone rings.

4. As soon as this rain stops, the girls (were practicing, will be practicing, practiced) their synchronized swimming routine.

5. Although Tom (was trying, is trying, will be trying) to stay out of trouble, his friends were always leading him astray.

6. We were enjoying the boat ride until the engine (was failing, will fail, failed).

7. Whenever the weather is warm, we (go, are going, were going) for a walk.

8. Customers (were buying, are buying, will be buying) tickets as the show started.

9. When the mayor (was pressing, pressed, will be pressing) the button, the first of the fireworks shot into the dark sky.

10. Throughout the picnic, bees and mosquitoes were attacking the picnickers, and all afternoon Gracie (apologized, apologizes, was apologizing) for choosing that spot.

D Check Up

Choose the verb or verb phrase that best completes each sentence.

1. While they wait for the spring thaw, gardeners _____ their gardens.

   A planned

   B are planning

   C planning

   D were planning

2. Perhaps, in coming decades, all students _____ at home in front of their computers.

   F stay

   G will stay

   H are staying

   J stayed

3. Every fall, supermarkets _____ turkeys and other foods for Thanksgiving.

   A advertise

   B advertising

   C are advertise

   D will advertising

4. Carrie _____ while she was standing in line.

   F will hum

   G is humming

   H was humming

   J hums

For each item, choose the sentence that is written correctly.

5. A Use of the pesticide DDT will be endangering wildlife after 1945.

   B For example, the chemical is causing pelicans to lay thin-shelled eggs that broke easily.

   C In 1972 the U.S. government will ban most uses of DDT.

   D After 1972, the number of pelicans in the U.S. increased.

6. F As Andrew was reading the newspaper, he is hearing odd noises overhead.

   G Squirrels running on his roof.

   H Andrew went outside and yells at the squirrels.

   J A neighbor who was walking past laughed at Andrew.

7. A Many people enjoy tales of Paul Bunyan, the giant lumberman.

   B The miner John Henry were the hero of tales and songs, as well.

   C Other folktales are tell about Pecos Bill, a cowboy, and Casey Jones, a railway engineer.

   D In the future, will a computer whiz being a hero of folklore?

8. F Although Cole Porter died in 1964, many of his songs still be popular today.

   G Porter was only eleven years old when his first song is published.

   H After he studied music in Paris, Porter wrote musicals.

   J Porter's best-known musical will be *Anything Goes*.

A Introduce

Perfect Tenses of Verbs

Perfect tenses express action completed by a certain time. Each perfect tense verb has at least two words: a simple tense form of *have* and the past participle of the main verb. The simple tense forms of *have* are the following: present—*has, have*; past—*had*; future—*will have*.

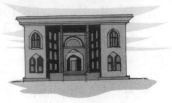

The **present perfect tense** is used to express action that began in the past. The action may be complete or continuing.

> The Noble Library <u>has served</u> the community for 50 years. (continuing action)
> Patrons <u>have approved</u> every library tax levy to date. (completed action)

The **past perfect tense** is used to express action that was completed before another action in the past.

> The Garden Club <u>had met</u> in private homes *before the new library building provided meeting rooms.*

The **future perfect tense** is used to express action that will be completed before a time or action in the future.

> The club <u>will have held</u> its 50th meeting in the library *by next June.*

Underline the verbs and verb phrases in each sentence. Write the perfect tense verbs on the lines.

1. I had dressed before I heard the weather report. _____

2. The directions for bike assembly look simple, but Eloise will have worked on the job for at least 40 hours by the time she gives it to Junior. _____

3. Tomás has already studied English for two months. _____

4. If you have not yet sent in your reservation, you may not get a seat.

   _____

5. Before the Capitol was opened in Washington, D.C., Congress had met in New York City. _____

6. Sweet Stuff will appear last on the program. By then, seven other bands will have played. _____

◆B◆ Practice

Circle the verb or verb phrase that best completes each sentence.

1. Stefan (worked, has worked) at that pizza parlor since high school.

2. Ever since the Liberty Bell cracked, no one (will have rung, has rung) it.

3. The U.S. economy (will have experienced, had experienced) major problems before the stock market crashed in 1929.

4. Last fall the local weather forecasters (have predicted, predicted) a dry winter.

5. Members of the machinists' union (have considered, will have considered) their options by the time they receive the company's offer.

6. Until Kristin finds a new apartment, she (will leave, will have left) her valuables at her parents' home.

7. Alfred (has painted, will have painted) Canadian nature scenes for sixteen years.

8. Robins (had built, built) nests in that tree before we put up the birdhouse.

9. Marie (bowled, has bowled) a perfect game last night at the *Rock 'n Bowl.*

10. Oh, no! I (will have found, have found) another historical error in this novel!

Underline the perfect tense verb in each of the following sentences.

11. Dan had read the *Chicago Tribune* every morning before he started reading the news on the Internet.

12. Juanita has enjoyed all of the band's concerts this year.

13. Joey will have traveled to fifteen different countries by the end of the month.

14. Both of my grandparents have lived in the same small neighborhood for fifty years.

15. Before Matthew bought his condominium, he had lived in Detroit with his parents.

16. By the time Christmas arrives, Jessica will have finished decorating her house in red and green.

17. Thomas had developed his own photographs before his brother-in-law bought him a digital camera.

18. The couple had gone to the farmer's market on Broadway every Saturday for three years.

C Apply

Read each pair of sentences. Circle the letter of the sentence that uses verb tenses correctly.

1. **A** The children have played in the pool before the thunder started.
   B The children had played in the pool before the thunder started.

2. **A** For centuries, Mexicans have honored dead relatives through special activities on the Day of the Dead.
   B For centuries, Mexicans are honored dead relatives through special activities on the Day of the Dead.

3. **A** Generations of Americans had developed their own version of the English language before Noah Webster produced the first American dictionary.
   B Generations of Americans had developed their own version of the English language before Noah Webster produces the first American dictionary.

4. **A** When this train arrived in Denver, it will have traveled for over nineteen hours.
   B When this train arrives in Denver, it will have traveled for over nineteen hours.

Complete each sentence with a perfect tense form of the verb in parentheses.

5. (build) Barely Good Enough Construction, Inc. _____ houses in this area before Mr. Mehta sued the company.

6. (plan) As of next March, Marianne _____ to remodel her kitchen for four years.

7. (use) Before the police caught him, the thief _____ counterfeit money in area stores.

8. (blow) A strong wind _____ all afternoon before the storm arrived.

9. (beat) Before losing last night's game, the Northern Lumber softball team

   _____ the East Side Auto team four times in a row.

10. (grow) Mike, I believe you _____ another foot taller since the last time I saw you!

Choose the verb or verb phrase that best completes each sentence.

1. Our family doctor retired because her malpractice insurance _____ too expensive.

   A has become

   B had become

   C will have become

   D becomes

2. That portrait _____ there for over 50 years.

   F has hung

   G have hung

   H will have hung

   J is hung

3. Ed _____ the book before his teacher recommended it.

   A have read

   B will have read

   C had read

   D has read

4. If he gets this batter out, the relief pitcher _____ his fourth game in five outings.

   F has saved

   G will has saved

   H will have saved

   J had saved

For each item, choose the sentence that is written correctly.

5. **A** Chan have camped in the woods for five summers.

   B This time, he develop a rash.

   C Before a doctor confirmed it, he knew that he had come into contact with poison ivy.

   D By tomorrow, he will have apply cortisone to his skin for a week.

6. **F** Election practices change over the past few decades.

   G Candidates has relied on personal appearances more before television commercials could speak for them.

   H Candidates have try to combat the public's distrust of politicians.

   J Election practices will have changed by the next century.

7. **A** Beverly and Debra have discussed possible problems before they decided to share an apartment.

   B Debra has never objected to housework while Beverly has always hated it.

   C While Debra cleans, Beverly has cooking for two.

   D By month's end, their arrangement will have be successful for two years.

8. **F** Ellen had never be on a plane before she started her new job.

   G Before the job switch, she had never even visited the East Coast.

   H Recently, however, she had meet with clients in Boston.

   J After her next trip, she will have flew 20,000 miles.

Agreement of Subjects and Verbs

The verb in a sentence must agree with its subject in number. In other words, a singular verb is used with a singular subject and a plural verb with a plural subject. Verbs in the present tense change form to show number.

Usually, the plural form of a verb is its present tense form.

>   Effective salespeople <u>show</u> the usefulness of their products.

The plural form of a verb is also used with *I* and *you*.

>   I <u>see</u> that you <u>have</u> the makings of a good salesman.

Almost always, the singular form of a verb is its present tense form plus *-s* or *-es*. This form is used only with a third-person singular subject. (Any subject that can be replaced with *he, she,* or *it* is third-person singular.)

>   Often a good dessert <u>disappears</u> in minutes.

Here are three exceptions to the above rules:

- The plural form of *be* is *are* (we are, you are, they are).

- *Be* has two singular forms, *am* and *is*. Use *am* with *I* (I am). Use *is* with third-person singular subjects (he is, she is, it is).

- The singular form of the verb *have* is *has* (he, she, or it has; they have).

Circle the subject and underline the correct verb form in parentheses. On the line, tell which form you chose. Write *S* for singular or *P* for plural.

1. The sun (rises, rise) in the east. _____

2. Several vines (climbs, climb) up the porch wall. _____

3. Scientists (searches, search) for the causes of illnesses. _____

4. In the next scene, an angry mob (gathers, gather) in the town square. _____

5. These questions (is, are) easy. _____

6. The curving walkway (leads, lead) to the back of the house. _____

7. Don't twist your wrist when you (lets, let) the ball go. _____

8. Because of the dangerous nature of cooking fires, kitchens (was, were) often built separate from the rest of the homes. _____

9. Usually, I (writes, write) with my right hand. _____

B Practice

In many sentences, a phrase describing the subject appears between the subject and the verb. The verb should agree with the subject, not the last word in the phrase.

> The <u>color</u> of those clouds <u>suggests</u> a coming storm. (The subject is *color*, a singular noun. The verb must be singular.)

> Lightning <u>flashes</u> splitting the sky <u>show</u> the arrival of a storm. (The subject is *flashes*, a plural noun. The verb must be plural.)

To choose the correct verb form in such a sentence, first find the subject. For the moment, ignore the words between the subject and the verb. Then choose the verb form that matches the subject.

> **Problem:** Rumbles of distant thunder (give, gives) a warning.

> **Process:** The subject is *Rumbles*. Think of the sentence as *Rumbles (give, gives) a warning.*

> **Solution:** Rumbles of distant thunder <u>give</u> a warning.

Circle the subject in each sentence. Then underline the correct verb form in parentheses.

1. A row of books (stands, stand) on each shelf of the bookcase.

2. Angry shouts coming from the restaurant kitchen (was, were) disturbing the diners.

3. (Does, Do) the movie end happily?

4. Tickets for the hit play (has, have) been sold out for weeks.

5. Jamal, the most talented player among our forwards, (thinks, think) of going pro.

6. Phone calls to the senator (was, were) strongly in favor of her stand.

7. Clues found at the crime scene (has, have) led investigators to suspect a former employee of the bank.

8. (Do, Does) the little girl see the parade from there?

9. All twelve members of the jury (agrees, agree) on the verdict.

10. Everyone in both Scout troops (likes, like) peanut butter.

11. All the students in the class (is, are) going on the field trip.

12. The dogs in the park (plays, play) happily every morning.

13. Strings of confetti (was, were) thrown at the bride and groom.

14. The children in the Smith family (has, have) the chicken pox.

 **Apply**

A **compound subject** has two or more parts. When the parts of a compound subject are joined by *and*, a plural verb is needed.

> <u>Peas</u> and <u>lettuce</u> *are* cold-weather crops.

When the parts of a compound subject are joined by *or* or *nor*, the verb agrees with the part closest to the verb.

> <u>Roses</u> or a <u>hibiscus</u> *is* my top choice for this sunny location. (The singular subject *hibiscus* is closer to the verb, so the verb is singular.)

> Neither the <u>skunk</u> nor the <u>squirrels</u> *have attacked* the garden—yet. (The plural subject *squirrels* is closer to the verb, so the helping verb is plural.)

In a few compound subjects, the two parts are considered as one whole. For example, "ham and eggs" names a single dish; so does "spaghetti and meatballs." In these rare cases, the compound subject takes a singular verb.

> <u>Spaghetti and meatballs</u> *is* an easy meal to prepare.

Circle each part of the compound subject in each sentence. Then underline the correct verb form in parentheses.

1. Either the crackers or the bread (am, is, are) on the second shelf.

2. Leah's gloves and her sweater (was, were) knitted by hand.

3. After such a heavy meal, neither the cake nor the cookies (appeals, appeal) to me.

4. Probably the children or their father (knows, know) how to program the VCR .

5. Believe me! Neither the ghost nor the scary monsters (is, are) real.

Underline the correct verb form in parentheses for each sentence.

6. Neither the famous storyteller nor his fans (copes, cope) well with real life.

7. Three small bowls or the single large one (fills, fill) the shelf.

8. Two twisted wheels and a bent bicycle frame (lies, lie) atop the rubbish pile.

9. In the parade, either the clowns or the elephant (follows, follow) the lion cage.

10. Neither Stanley nor his brothers (runs, run) very fast.

11. Both the vases of flowers and the oval rug (brightens, brighten) the drab room.

12. Often, wooden shoes or a windmill (represents, represent) Holland in children's books.

D Check Up

Choose the verb or verb phrase that best completes each sentence.

1. This old vacuum cleaner _____ much of the dirt on the carpet.

   A will have left

   B have left

   C leaves

   D leave

2. This sports interviewer very rarely _____ the tough questions.

   F ask

   G have asked

   H asks

   J will have asked

3. Every day, either Gladys or her daughters _____ the dog for a walk.

   A takes

   B take

   C will have taken

   D has taken

4. Neither raindrops nor sunshine _____ a way through these blinds.

   F finds

   G have found

   H find

   J will have found

For each item, choose the sentence in which the subject and verb agree.

5. A A strong beginning do not always guarantee a successful end to a project.

   B The two pianos in the school's storeroom has finally been tuned.

   C Neither the CEO nor his staff members provide good reasons for the company's problems.

   D Both the antique lamps and the new vase is extremely delicate.

6. F Either your grandparents or your aunt has your photo album.

   G An assortment of fragrant candles make a nice housewarming gift.

   H Do a second pillowcase come with the set of sheets?

   J Alex's buddies and he bowls on Wednesday evening.

7. A Several cowboys and a stagecoach appears in the background of the painting.

   B Avoid this meter because some coins or perhaps paper money are stuck in the slot.

   C Neither Carolyn nor the other secretaries works overtime.

   D The phonograph, like 78-rpm records, is ancient history.

8. F Has you or Maxine seen the new horror movie?

   G Sharpened pencils and a notebook are necessary supplies.

   H Wood sold in some of the discount stores seem to be of inferior quality.

   J Louis love to play basketball.

A Introduce

Easily Confused Verbs

It is easy to confuse some pairs of verbs because their meanings are so similar or they sound so much alike. Memorize the meanings and the principal parts of these verbs so you can use the words correctly.

Rise and *Raise:* *Raise* means "to lift." *Rise* means "to go up."

Present	Past	Past Participle
raise	raised	raised
rise	rose	risen

Set and *Sit:* *Set* means "to place (something)." *Sit* means "to rest (in a chair)."

Present	Past	Past Participle
sit	sat	sat
set	set	set

Accept and *Except:* These words are often confused because they sound so much alike. *Accept* means "to take or receive willingly." The principal parts of *accept* follow regular rules. *Except*, in its common use as a preposition, means "other than" or "leaving out."

> The baseball team's manager refused to <u>accept</u> defeat.
> Everyone <u>except</u> the manager thought the team would lose.

Complete each sentence by writing the principal part described in parentheses.

1. (present of *sit*) I like to _____ in the bleachers to watch the game.

2. (past of *accept*) Joann _____ her diploma and walked off the stage.

3. (past participle of *rise*) The temperature had _____ to 90 degrees by noon.

4. (past of *sit*) Erin _____ under the tree and read her book.

5. (past participle of *set*) The family had _____ their best china on the table.

6. (past of *raise*) Aaron _____ a bucket of water from the old well.

7. (present of *accept*) When you _____ a job, you promise to do your best.

8. (past of *rise*) The spectators _____ when the judge entered the courtroom.

9. (present of *set*) Those noises _____ my teeth on edge.

B Practice

Have and *Of:* Some people run into trouble when they write the verb *have* with a helping verb such as *could*, *would*, or *should*. Because speakers don't always speak clearly, the phrases often end up sounding like *could of, would of,* or *should of,* or even *could a, would a,* or *should a.* These spellings of the phrases are never correct in formal writing.

Correct: We <u>should have</u> gotten off the freeway at the last exit.

Wrong: We <u>should of</u> gotten off the freeway at the last exit.

For each item, circle the letter of the sentence in which the verb is used correctly.

1. **A** Gene would of helped us move if he hadn't hurt his back.
   B Gene would have helped us move if he hadn't hurt his back.

2. **A** Everyone except Marty had learned how to ice-skate.
   B Everyone accept Marty had learned how to ice-skate.

3. **A** If you set with your head between your knees, you will feel better.
   B If you sit with your head between your knees, you will feel better.

4. **A** I raised the window, but it fell back down again.
   B I rised the window, but it fell back down again.

5. **A** After Amanda sat the groceries down, she answered the phone.
   B After Amanda set the groceries down, she answered the phone.

6. **A** I except the office of mayor of this great city.
   B I accept the office of mayor of this great city.

Complete each sentence by underlining the correct word in parentheses.

7. (Set, Sit) a placecard in front of every plate.

8. Just before the sun (rises, raises), the birds begin to sing.

9. Janice has (sat, set) a bowl of milk out for the stray cat.

10. Please (except, accept) my apology for the misunderstanding.

11. The shipment shouldn't (of, have) been left without a signature.

12. Karl (set, sat) in the doctor's office for over an hour.

C Apply

Read each sentence. If you find a verb used incorrectly, rewrite the sentence correctly on the line. If the sentence is written properly, write *Correct* on the line.

1. The seller excepted the offer, so the house is ours!

   _____

2. I would of helped you, if I had known you were in trouble.

   _____

3. The movers sat the boxes on the dining room floor.

   _____

4. The grocery store has risen the prices on their name brand items.

   _____

5. I accept the nomination for president of the club.

   _____

6. Don't raise my hopes if you aren't going to follow through.

   _____

7. You should not of been playing catch inside the house.

   _____

8. Driving was made dangerous by the dense fog that had raised.

   _____

9. All the kittens accept the small calico have been adopted.

   _____

10. The old mansion sets on a hill overlooking the valley.

    _____

11. After the children had sat quietly for ten minutes, they became impatient.

    _____

12. Our team would a won if we had kicked a field goal.

    _____

D Check Up

For each item, choose the sentence that is written correctly.

1. **A** The grandfather clock had set in the same spot for thirty years.

   B On weekdays, Rita sets her alarm for six o'clock.

   C My dog sets by the door and waits for me after work.

   D I know I sat my wallet on the nightstand last night.

2. **F** We should of known that it would rain on our picnic.

   G If I had left early, we might not of met.

   H Dan would have met you at the airport if he had known your flight number.

   J I shouldn't a counted on getting a raise.

3. **A** The price of a gallon of milk has risen over the last month.

   B Our club has risen over one thousand dollars for local charities.

   C Tonight, the moon will raise at ten o'clock.

   D A cloud of steam raised above the sidewalk grate.

4. **F** I can't except such an expensive gift from you.

   G Nancy had planned for every possibility accept the one that actually happened.

   H No one accept you knows my secret.

   J This store does not accept credit cards.

5. **A** The wolf's howl raised mournfully into the night air.

   B You have risen a son you can be proud of.

   C The singer raised her voice to be heard over the orchestra.

   D Please help me rise this mirror just a little.

6. **F** Please except this token of our appreciation.

   G The maid will do any job except washing the windows.

   H This parking meter will not except pennies.

   J Julie has been to every state accept Alaska and Hawaii.

7. **A** I shouldn't a read the last pages of the book first.

   B Sally could of been working on the project all week.

   C I should of ordered a salad instead of a sandwich.

   D We couldn't have completed the project on time without your help.

8. **F** Please sit the books on the table by the window.

   G Wendy was tired of sitting at a computer all day.

   H Setting in the comfortable easy chair, Leo fell asleep.

   J The enemies have sat aside their differences and agreed to a compromise.

Adjectives

A modifier is a word that describes other words or limits their meaning in some way. Adjectives modify nouns or pronouns. **Adjectives** describe *which one, what kind,* or *how many.*

> The <u>large cardboard</u> box contained <u>three</u> pizzas.
> (*Large* and *cardboard* describe box. *Three* describes *pizzas.*)

Adjectives change their form when the word they modify is used in a comparison. If the adjective has only one or two syllables, add *-er* to compare two things. Add *-est* to compare three or more things.

> Chihuahuas are <u>smaller</u> than collies. (comparative form; describes *chihuahuas*)
> Chihuahuas are the <u>smallest</u> of all dogs. (superlative form; describes *chihuahuas*)

If the adjective has two or more syllables, use *more* or *less* to compare two things. Use *most* or *least* to compare three or more things.

> My new shoes are <u>more comfortable</u> than my old ones. (comparative form)
> These are the <u>most comfortable</u> shoes I've ever worn. (superlative form)

Use just one form of an adjective in a comparison.

> **Wrong:** Today is <u>more hotter</u> than yesterday.
> **Right:** Today is <u>hotter</u> than yesterday.

Underline the adjectives in the following sentences.

1. Raoul's new boat is larger than his old one.

2. Every spring, yellow dandelions cover my entire lawn.

3. The restaurant had three cozy booths and several round tables.

4. The weather forecast called for heavy rain and high winds.

5. Are dolphins more intelligent than porpoises?

6. After the fierce storm, a rainbow appeared in the blue sky.

7. We needed four gallons of oak stain to finish the wooden deck.

8. Frugal Marie chose the least expensive dinner on the menu.

9. Ted is happier since he changed jobs.

10. Pick only the ripest and juiciest peaches off the trees.

B Practice

Before adding *-er* or *-est* to an adjective, follow these rules:

- If the adjective is a one syllable word with a short vowel and a single consonant at the end, double the final consonant.

  thi<u>n</u>   thi<u>nn</u>er

- If the adjective ends in *e*, drop the final *e*.

  hug<u>e</u>   hugest

- If the adjective ends in a consonant and *y*, change the *y* to *i*.

  earl<u>y</u>   earlier

A few adjectives do not follow the usual pattern. For these adjectives, the whole word changes to make the comparative and superlative forms.

| good | better | best | bad | worse | worst |
| many | more | most | little | less | least |

For each item, write the correct form of the adjective.

1. comparative form of *lovely*   _____

2. superlative form of *dull*   _____

3. superlative form of *bashful*   _____

4. superlative form of *bad*   _____

5. comparative form of *beautiful*   _____

6. superlative form of *close*   _____

7. comparative form of *flat*   _____

Read each sentence. If the underlined adjective is not correct, write the proper form on the line. If there is no mistake, write *Correct* on the line.

8. Are Kayla's eyes <u>more bluer</u> than her brother's? _____

9. Cornell is the <u>shortest</u> player on the basketball team. _____

10. This pie is <u>more better</u> than the last one I baked. _____

11. The statue was wrapped in <u>many</u> layers of packing than the book.

    _____

12. The <u>smallest</u> of the two horses won the race. _____

C ◆ Apply

Use the correct form of the adjective in parentheses to complete each sentence.

1. (fast) Mrs. Wolf worked the _____ of all the hospital volunteers.

2. (rusty) The right side of your car looks _____ than the left side.

3. (fresh) Please inspect the _____ vegetables carefully.

4. (large) Who grew the _____ tomatoes at the community garden?

5. (cheap) Is this battery _____ than the last one I purchased?

6. (desirable) In my opinion, blueberry muffins are _____ than pancakes for breakfast.

7. (powerful) Personal computers are _____ than they were previously.

8. (dressy) Bernice chose the _____ outfit in the entire store.

9. (healthy) Which salad is _____, the fruit or the mixed greens?

10. (long) The Great Barrier Reef is the _____ coral reef in the world.

11. (great) _____ flocks of geese swam in the river.

12. (expensive) Did Sue select the _____ ring she could afford?

13. (good) Waffles are good, but bagels are _____.

14. (pretty) Choose the _____ basket of the four.

15. (hairy) Mr. Reed's dog is very _____.

Choose one of the following groups and imagine one particular member of that group. What details set it off from all other members of the group? For example, if the group was months, what makes December different from the other months of the year? Write a description that includes at least eight adjectives. Circle the adjectives.

hot-air balloons   dogs   cars   jackets   houseplants

_____

_____

_____

_____

D ▸ Check Up

Look at the underlined adjective in each sentence. Choose the answer that is written correctly for the adjective.

1. Compact cars are <u>least costly</u> than vans.

   A least costlier

   B less costly

   C less costlier

   D Correct as it is

2. Does this toothpaste actually make your teeth <u>whiter</u> within a few days?

   F more whiter

   G whitest

   H most white

   J Correct as it is

3. <u>Fewest</u> people came than were expected.

   A Few

   B More fewer

   C Fewer

   D Correct as it is

4. Sizzling Steak House serves the <u>more thick</u> sirloin steaks in the city.

   F thicker

   G thick

   H thickest

   J Correct as it is

5. Tom had <u>little</u> luck at guessing my age.

   A less

   B least

   C lesser

   D Correct as it is

6. We're anticipating a <u>worst</u> blizzard today than we had yesterday.

   F worse

   G more worse

   H badder

   J Correct as it is

7. Reese is the <u>most enthusiastic</u> worker on the assembly line.

   A enthusiastic

   B more enthusiastic

   C enthusiasticest

   D Correct as it is

8. To repair the phone, Antonio needed a <u>thin</u> cable than he had with him.

   F more thinner

   G thinest

   H thinner

   J Correct as it is

Adverbs

Adverbs are words that modify verbs, adjectives, or other adverbs. They describe *how, when, where,* or *to what degree.* They may add a positive or negative meaning to the words they modify. Many adverbs end in *-ly.*

> The <u>very</u> unreliable truck <u>almost never</u> runs <u>smoothly</u> on the road. (*Very* describes the adjective *unreliable; almost* describes the adverb *never; never* and *smoothly* describes the verb *runs.*)

In comparisons, adverbs follow the same pattern as adjectives. If an adverb has one or two syllables, add *-er* to compare two actions or *-est* to compare three or more actions. Most adverbs with two syllables or more use *more* or *less* for the comparative form and *most* or *least* for the superlative form.

> Jamie and Sue arrived <u>earlier</u> than the other couple. (describes the verb *arrived*)
> Of all the data entry clerks, Felicia works <u>most accurately</u>. (describes the verb *works*)

Find the adverb in each sentence. Write it on the line. Remember that some adverbs may include *more, less, most,* or *least*.

1. _____ Paul swung lazily in the oversized hammock.

2. _____ Because we were busy, we scarcely had time to eat.

3. _____ Acme Company recently hired five new workers.

4. _____ Hsu volunteered for the difficult assignments more often than anyone else did.

5. _____ The raging fire completely destroyed the warehouse.

6. _____ Is the antique mall open daily?

7. _____ Within the family, Madelaine felt the loss of Aunt Jane most deeply.

8. _____ The audience waited expectantly for the concert to begin.

9. _____ That was an unusually rough stretch of highway!

10. _____ Louise was not surprised by all the attention she received.

B Practice

To spell the comparative and superlative forms of adverbs, follow the same rules as for adjectives.

> Lucy tried <u>hard</u> to get the singers' autographs. She arrived at the concert <u>early</u> and sat <u>close</u> to the stage.

> hard hard<u>er</u> hard<u>est</u>   early earl<u>ier</u> earl<u>iest</u>   close clos<u>er</u> clos<u>est</u>

Some adverbs follow a special form for comparisons.

> well better best   badly worse worst
> much more most   little less least

Use just one form of the adverb in a comparison.

> **Wrong:** Miguel walked <u>more faster</u> than Inez.

> **Right:** Miguel walked <u>faster</u> than Inez.

Write each of the adverbs below under the correct heading on the chart.

> least   more evenly   daily   later   most efficiently
> never   most bravely   better   scarcely

Adverbs	Comparative Forms	Superlative Forms
_____	_____	_____
_____	_____	_____
_____	_____	_____

Underline the adverb in each sentence. If the form is incorrect, write it correctly on the line. If there are no mistakes, write _Correct_ on the line.

10. Danika quickly found the error and corrected it. _____

11. Tony scores baskets more better than any of his teammates do.

    _____

12. We lived the most farthest from our job. _____

13. Dirt partially covered the old chest. _____

14. The engineer most badly underestimated the cost. _____

15. Brandon slipped away from the party earliest. _____

16. Morgan performs most best when not under pressure. _____

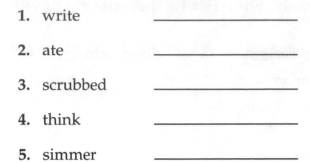

C ▸ Apply

Write an adverb that modifies each verb below. The adverb should describe how, when, or where the action takes place.

1. write _____

2. ate _____

3. scrubbed _____

4. think _____

5. simmer _____

Write an adverb that modifies the underlined adjective or adverb in each phrase below.

6. _____ <u>rugged</u> mountain

7. _____ <u>recently</u> acquired car

8. _____ <u>important</u> data

9. _____ <u>false</u> statement

10. _____ <u>always</u> does

Complete each sentence by adding an adverb. Use the proper form for any comparison.

11. Decide _____ on the proper course of action.

12. Heather speaks so _____ it is difficult to hear her.

13. Marcus repaired my car _____ than the other mechanic did.

14. Have you _____ gone ice fishing?

15. This library book is due _____.

16. Mr. O'Conner flies _____ of all the salesmen in our division.

17. He had _____ begun painting when the phone rang.

18. The crowd cheered _____ when the home team entered the field.

19. Our new alarm clock rings _____ than our old one did.

20. My youngest daughter calls _____ of all my children.

D Check Up

Look at the underlined word or words in each sentence. Choose the answer that is written correctly for the underlined part.

1. Shake the bottle <u>most vigorously</u> to mix the contents.

   A most vigorous

   B more vigorously

   C vigorously

   D Correct as it is

2. We couldn't believe how <u>easy</u> the problem was solved.

   F easily

   G most easily

   H more easily

   J Correct as it is

3. It seemed <u>most</u> likely that Paula would receive the promotion rather than Rita.

   A much

   B more

   C mostly

   D Correct as it is

4. Of all the cars I've owned, this one requires repairs <u>least often</u>.

   F less often

   G little often

   H least oftenest

   J Correct as it is

5. Because of her sprained ankle, Tamika limped <u>bad</u> for several weeks.

   A worse

   B worst

   C badly

   D Correct as it is

6. Rolf spoke <u>less confidently</u> than he had the last time we met.

   F confidently

   G least confidently

   H less confident

   J Correct as it is

7. Mr. Lovejoy wrote <u>more movingly</u> about his plans for the future.

   A movingly

   B most moving

   C movinglier

   D Correct as it is

8. This engine will perform <u>more well</u> if it is cleaned regularly.

   F good

   G more better

   H better

   J Correct as it is

Adjective or Adverb?

Both adjectives and adverbs modify other words. Sometimes the same word is used as an adjective in one sentence and as an adverb in another.

> The <u>early</u> movie begins at 4 o'clock. (adjective, tells what kind)
> She arrived <u>early</u> this morning. (adverb, tells when)

The comparative and superlative forms of the adjective *good* and the adverb *well* look the same:

adjective: good   better   best
adverb: well   better   best

Even though there are likenesses in appearance, remember the differences, especially in use, between the two types of modifiers.

Adjectives	**Adverbs**
• Describe nouns or pronouns	• Describe verbs, adjectives, or other adverbs
• Tell *which one, what kind,* or *how many*	• Tell *how, when, where,* or *to what degree*
	• Many, but not all, end in *-ly*

Read each sentence. Circle the word modified by the underlined word. If the underlined word is an adjective, write *ADJ* on the line. If the word is an adverb, write *ADV*.

1. This bus is late <u>almost</u> every morning. _____

2. Mary <u>suddenly</u> slipped on the worn stair. _____

3. My nephew is a <u>timid</u> fellow. _____

4. The project started <u>well</u>, but problems soon developed. _____

5. We work at a <u>hectic</u> pace, so we are tired at the end of the day. _____

6. After changing the oil in her car, Joyce's hands were <u>grimy</u>. _____

7. Ms. Greene responded <u>coolly</u> to the last-minute invitation. _____

8. He felt <u>better</u> prepared for the questions than he had been last time. _____

9. Julio works the <u>late</u> shift at Glenview Hospital. _____

10. Who is the <u>most capable</u> person for the new job opening? _____

11. After the long walk, Jim's dog <u>thirstily</u> lapped the water. _____

B Practice

Adding -ly to a descriptive adjective that tells *what kind* changes the word to an adverb that describes *how*. Here are some examples:

Adjective	Adverb
fierce	fiercely
lucky	luckily
honest	honestly

When these adjectives and adverbs are used in comparisons, their forms have clear differences. Study the following examples:

Adjective	Adverb
fierce, fiercer, fiercest	fiercely, more fiercely, most fiercely
lucky, luckier, luckiest	luckily, more luckily, most luckily
honest, more honest, most honest	honestly, more honestly, most honestly

First determine whether an adjective or an adverb is needed. Then, if the modifier is used in a comparison, choose between the comparative and superlative forms.

Circle the correct modifier in each sentence.

1. He gave (most generous, most generously) of all to the scholarship fund.

2. Purchase the (most darkly, darkest) curtain you can find.

3. The river is (more peaceful, more peacefully) here than it is downstream.

4. We (wise, wisely) decided to skip the appetizer and get dessert instead.

5. If you speak (firmer, more firmly) than that, your dog will obey you.

6. To make a (good, well) impression at the job interview, dress appropriately.

7. It is (more easily, easier) to leave the freeway here than to drive to the next exit.

8. Arnie's truck jolted (abrupt, abruptly) to a stop.

9. My sister speaks Chinese (more fluent, more fluently) than I do.

10. They divided the bill as (fair, fairly) as possible.

11. Jacob speaks (good, well) but has some trouble with writing.

12. When the lights went out, my young son was (more fearful, more fearfully) than I was.

13. Who is the (most loyally, most loyal) member of the civic association?

C ▸ Apply

Use the adjective or the adverb written in boldface to complete each sentence.
Change the word to comparative or superlative form if necessary.

patient   patiently

1. Treena _____ coaxed her son to finish the meal.

2. Are you _____ with strangers than with family members?

3. Alex is the _____ person in the group.

high   highly

4. Who is the _____ acclaimed singer in the world?

5. Will the person with the _____ score win the contest?

6. It is _____ unlikely that we'll see each other soon.

quiet   quietly

7. The library is a _____ place for students to study.

8. Moira is _____ in history class than her twin sister Maura.

9. Jody is _____ making plans for her husband's surprise birthday party.

Use a form of the adjective or adverb in parentheses to complete each sentence.

10. (soon) Henry finished the task _____ than the other plumber.

11. (loud) When Bella saw the snake, she shrieked _____.

12. (kind) Mrs. Fioretti is the _____ woman I've ever met.

13. (early) Will the office open _____ because of the volume of work?

14. (soft) Talk _____ so you do not frighten the sleeping child.

15. (brave) The doe _____ defended her fawn from the wolves.

16. (careful) Alicia listened _____ to the manager's directions.

17. (good) Which road is _____, Highway 12 or Route 306?

18. (excellent) From this list of restaurants, choose the one with the

_____ service.

D Check Up

For each item, choose the sentence that uses adjectives and adverbs correctly.

1. A Sam is the most thoughtfully person in the office.

   B During the chess match, Daniel made boldest plays than his opponent.

   C Our vacation passed too rapid.

   D The lawyer skillfully argued the case in court.

2. F Is the poetry of Langston Hughes as well known as that of Robert Frost?

   G Dr. Biggs careful examined his patient.

   H Do you exercise on a regularly basis?

   J The Great Plains have vastly areas of prairie land.

3. A Bob is the most carelessly person I know.

   B Walking along the beach is the most peaceful activity of my busy life.

   C Vanessa plays the trumpet good.

   D The sudden rain brought least relief from the heat.

4. F One candidate spoke more forceful than the other.

   G Jeffrey volunteered cheerful to lead the clean-up crew.

   H The foundation is the most solid part of the building.

   J Our puppy fearless defended her squeaky toy from the cat.

Look at the underlined word or words in each sentence. Choose the answer that is written correctly for the underlined part.

5. Because I walked <u>most fastest</u> than James, I finished the course first.

   A fastest

   B fastly

   C faster

   D Correct as it is

6. Her <u>gentle</u> voice soothed the restless child.

   F gently

   G gentler

   H more gently

   J Correct as it is

7. Philip <u>recent</u> returned from the Peace Corps.

   A recently

   B more recently

   C most recent

   D Correct as it is

8. Yolanda is <u>highest</u> creative in designing new computer games.

   F most highest

   G highly

   H most highly

   J Correct as it is

Using Negative Words Correctly

When you talk with friends or family, your speech may not always follow the rules of formal language, also known as standard English. When you are at work or in formal situations, however, you are expected to follow those rules. One rule of standard English is to avoid using more than one negative word in a sentence or clause. Such an error is called using a **double negative.**

> My dog <u>never</u> bit <u>nobody</u> before.

Most negative words include the word *no*. Here are some common negative words:

no	nobody	not	nowhere	barely	scarcely
no one	none	nothing	never	hardly	

Other negative words are the contractions that end in *n't.*

One negative word communicates your message adequately. When you want to correct a double negative, just take away all but one of the negative words.

> **Double negative:** I <u>can't</u> <u>hardly</u> tell you how sorry I am.
> **Standard:** I can <u>hardly</u> tell you how sorry I am.
> **Standard:** I <u>can't</u> tell you how sorry I am.

Read each sentence. If it uses negative words incorrectly, circle the negative words. If the negative words are used correctly, write *C* on the line.

1. _____ I could scarcely find nobody to help me weed the garden.

2. _____ Timmy can't never sit still long enough to read a whole book.

3. _____ The critic could find nothing wrong with the orchestra's performance.

4. _____ If no one bids higher, the antique quilt will be sold to you.

5. _____ Since his accident, Sean has vowed never to try nothing risky again.

6. _____ There isn't no way that I could be responsible for the mix-up.

7. _____ Traci couldn't find her car nowhere in the parking lot.

8. _____ The committee didn't come up with no new ideas for the project.

9. _____ Why doesn't nothing ever go the way I plan it?

10. _____ The van could barely make its way up the snowy hill.

B Practice

Underline the word that correctly completes each sentence.

1. Moira hadn't seen (none, any) of the films that were nominated.
2. The director hasn't (ever, never) worked with that actress before.
3. The Hull family didn't go (anywhere, nowhere) on vacation this year.
4. Can't you drive to the airport (any, no) faster?
5. Didn't (nobody, anybody) bring a can opener?
6. Ken doesn't want (no one, anyone) disturbing his desk while he is away.
7. The singer (could, couldn't) barely reach the high notes in the song.
8. There (were, weren't) hardly enough handouts for everyone at the meeting.
9. Delia won't let (anything, nothing) spoil her son's birthday party.
10. There's never (no, any) good reason to tell a lie.

In each item, the first sentence has a double negative. Circle the letter of the sentence that corrects the double negative.

11. I couldn't barely read the tiny print at the bottom of the application.
    A I could barely read the tiny print at the bottom of the application.
    B I couldn't hardly read the tiny print at the bottom of the application.

12. The young patient couldn't scarcely swallow the big pill.
    A The young patient could scarcely swallow the big pill.
    B The young patient couldn't swallow no big pill.

13. Trisha didn't find no one to buy her old kitchen table.
    A Trisha didn't never find anyone to buy her old kitchen table.
    B Trisha found no one to buy her old kitchen table.

14. The abandoned factory isn't being maintained properly no more.
    A The abandoned factory isn't hardly being maintained properly anymore.
    B The abandoned factory isn't being maintained properly anymore.

15. Nothing will never be decided if we continue to argue.
    A Nothing will ever be decided if we continue to argue.
    B Nothing won't ever be decided if we continue to argue.

C ⟩ Apply

Read each sentence. If it contains a double negative, rewrite it correctly. If it is written properly, write *Correct* on the line.

1. The coffee was barely cool enough to drink.

   _____

2. Alicia couldn't find nowhere to hang the huge poster.

   _____

3. This project can't, in no way, be considered a failure.

   _____

4. Doesn't anybody remember the words to my favorite show's theme song?

   _____

5. I never asked for nothing for dessert.

   _____

6. There is scarcely enough time to get to the theater before the movie starts.

   _____

Each of the following sentences has a double negative. Write two sentences on the lines. Each new sentence should correct the double negative in a different way.

7. Laura won't never fit into that jacket again.

   _____

   _____

8. The principal can't make no exceptions to the school rules.

   _____

   _____

9. Fresh strawberries aren't available in none of the grocery stores today.

   _____

   _____

For each item, choose the sentence that uses negative words correctly.

1. **A** Rene never forgets no one's birthday.

   B We can't fit any more packages in this truck.

   C Nobody here knows nothing about how to work this machine.

   D Kim couldn't hardly wait to tell her parents the good news.

2. **F** Please don't try to make no excuses for the blunder.

   G The lookout could barely see the island in the distance.

   H Devon doesn't never lose his temper on the job.

   J There wasn't no bell to ring, so the delivery person knocked.

3. **A** Tina hasn't ever learned how to roller-skate.

   B There wasn't scarcely any cereal left in the box this morning.

   C Some people won't ever try nothing new or different.

   D The stranded motorist couldn't get no one to help him.

4. **F** My sister is scarcely never on time for anything.

   G It doesn't do no good to tell me that you're sorry now.

   H I didn't have no time to eat breakfast this morning.

   J Craig has never traveled anywhere in Europe.

Read the paragraph and look at the numbered, underlined words. Choose the answer that is written correctly for each set of underlined words.

(5)   How foods look is nearly as important as how they taste. <u>Hardly nobody would</u> object to eating a shiny red apple or a green salad. But you probably
(6) <u>wouldn't have no</u> desire to eat blue mashed potatoes, even if they really
(7) <u>didn't have nothing</u> wrong with them. Maybe our reaction to blue foods is a built-in
(8) protection that we have developed over the centuries to insure we <u>don't eat any</u> moldy foods.

5. **A** Hardly anybody would

   B Nobody wouldn't

   C Hardly anybody wouldn't

   D Correct as it is

6. **F** wouldn't have none

   G wouldn't have barely any

   H would have no

   J Correct as it is

7. **A** never had nothing

   B didn't have hardly anything

   C had nothing

   D Correct as it is

8. **F** don't eat no

   G don't never eat

   H never eat no

   J Correct as it is

Review

Nouns

A **noun** is a word that names a person, place, or thing. Nouns can be singular or plural. **Common nouns** are general names of any persons, places, or things. **Proper nouns** are the names of particular persons, places, or things. Begin each important word in a proper noun with a capital letter.

Pronouns

Pronouns are words used in place of nouns. Pronouns must agree with their **antecedents** (the nouns they replace) in number, gender, and person.

Verbs

A verb is a word that names an action or a state of being. **Action verbs** may be active or passive. Verbs that express a state of being, such as *is, are, was,* or *were*, may be **linking verbs. Helping verbs**, such as *will, can,* and *must,* are used along with action or linking verbs.

To show when an action happens, the form of a verb changes. The different forms are called **tenses.** The simple tenses are present, past, and future. There are also perfect tenses and progressive tenses.

Every verb must agree with its subject in number.

Adjectives and Adverbs

An **adjective** is a word that modifies a noun or a pronoun. Adjectives tell *which one, what kind,* or *how many.* Adverbs modify verbs, adjectives, and other adverbs. **Adverbs** answer the question *how, when, where,* or *to what degree.* Many adverbs end in *-ly.* Adjectives and adverbs change their forms when they are used in comparisons.

Negative Words

According to the rules of standard English, speakers and writers should avoid using two negative words in the same clause or sentence. Negative words include the following: *no, not, never, hardly, scarcely, barely,* and all contractions made using the word *not.* To correct a double negative, remove one of the negative words.

Choose the word that correctly completes each sentence.

1. If you don't want all _____ French fries, I'd be glad to finish them.

   A you're

   B your

   C yours

   D you

2. When you see Greg, remind _____ about the meeting.

   F him

   G he

   H them

   J his

3. Tomorrow morning Shane _____ his cross-country bike ride.

   A had begun

   B begin

   C began

   D will begin

4. The workers _____ own stock in the company.

   F themselfs

   G themselves

   H theirselves

   J ourselfs

5. By the time Meg reaches the shore, she _____ for almost an hour.

   A will swim

   B swims

   C will have swum

   D swam

6. Both sisters had _____ mother's blue eyes.

   F their

   G ours

   H theirs

   J her

7. The consultant told _____ that our plant was inefficient.

   A he

   B she

   C us

   D we

8. Last night the team _____ the best game of the season.

   F play

   G plays

   H will play

   J played

9. This year's peaches are even _____ than last year's.

   A more deliciously

   B most deliciously

   C more delicious

   D most delicious

10. You'll have to speak _____ if you want to be heard over the machines.

    F more louder

    G more loudly

    H loudest

    J most loudest

For each item, choose the sentence that is written correctly.

11. A Everyone accept Hector has seen the hit movie.

    B I accept this award on behalf of the winner, who could not be here today.

    C Will you except a reward for finding my dog?

    D Kia enjoys all kinds of music accept fusion jazz.

12. F Dave carved a Halloween pumpkin for his children.

    G We will plan a party that was held last Saturday.

    H Many customers complains about high prices.

    J I wait by the phone until you called.

13. A That book about quilts are shelved in the main room.

    B Parties for the president's inauguration was well attended.

    C Tickets for the show is still available at the box office.

    D Our group of operators is ready to take your call.

14. F These bird of prey is quite rare.

    G Who gave Yolanda this toys for her birthday?

    H This is one of those games in which you act out a book or movie title.

    J The ambulance came from those fire station.

15. A Can you tell me the quickest way to get downtown?

    B I need to get to the meeting more earlier than the clients.

    C I dressed more careful than usual this morning.

    D This could be the more important meeting of the whole year.

16. F Either the mayor or her aides is expected at the rally.

    G Both the suburbs and downtown is experiencing a severe water shortage.

    H Representatives from the county offers ideas to solve the problem.

    J Residents of the city find these meetings helpful.

17. A The boys set on the porch steps and looked at the stars.

    B The mail carrier sat the package by the back door.

    C That statue has sat in the same place for over ten years.

    D If you set down on the park bench now, you will get wet.

18. F I would of forgotten the meeting if you hadn't reminded me.

    G Wanda may have filed those papers in this cabinet.

    H Those checks should a been sent out last week.

    J I might of left the tickets in my other coat!

Read the following passages and look at their numbered, underlined parts. Choose the answer that is written correctly for each underlined part.

The elegant "cottages" of Newport, Rhode Island, are some of the
(19) <u>most beautifulest</u> homes in the United States. The owners who built them
(20) <u>didn't spare no</u> expense. To impress their friends and clients, they go to the
(21) buildings of Europe for inspiration. One of the houses <u>has built</u> to look like the
(22) home of French king Louis XIV. Another Newport home popular with visitors <u>feature</u>
rooms that were constructed entirely in Europe and shipped to the United States.

19. **A** most beautiful

    B most beautifully

    C beautifulest

    D Correct as it is

20. **F** didn't spare hardly any

    G didn't spare none

    H spared no

    J Correct as it is

21. **A** have built

    B was built

    C are built

    D Correct as it is

22. **F** will feature

    G feature

    H features

    J Correct as it is

(23)   Little Ally took her first step yesterday. She wanted to get to <u>their</u> Aunt Joan,
(24) <u>which</u> was sitting across the room. So, without thinking, she put one foot in front
(25) of the other and started walking! Everyone <u>accept</u> me started clapping. Ally was
(26) so shocked at all the commotion that she just <u>sat</u> right down in the middle of the
room and started crying.

23. **A** her

    B his

    C hers

    D Correct as it is

24. **F** that

    G who

    H whose

    J Correct as it is

25. **A** excepts

    B accepts

    C except

    D Correct as it is

26. **F** set

    G sit

    H sets

    J Correct as it is

A Introduce

Complete Sentences and Fragments

A complete sentence must include both a subject and a predicate. The **subject** names the person or thing that is doing something. The **predicate**, which always includes a verb, tells what the subject is doing.

My grandfather   <u>started</u> his own plumbing business.
subject   predicate (The verb is underlined.)

In commands, the subject *you* is often not stated but understood.

(You)   <u>Sit</u> down over there.
subject   predicate (The verb is underlined.)

Here are two types of **sentence fragments** and a way to correct each one.

1. To correct a fragment with a subject but no predicate, add a predicate.

   Fragment: Eight of the students.
   Correction: Eight of the students <u>went home sick</u>.

2. To correct a fragment with a predicate but no subject, add a subject.

   Fragment: Used to be a professional dancer.
   Correction: <u>Boris</u> used to be a professional dancer.

Write *CS* beside each complete sentence. Underline its subject once and circle its predicate. Write *F* beside each fragment.

1. _____ Mrs. Munson owns the laundromat on Fourth Street.

2. _____ Tossed her keys out the window.

3. _____ The black cat with a white patch on its chest.

4. _____ My brother is moving to Alaska.

5. _____ Michelle's daughter from her first marriage.

6. _____ The new movie theater opened last Friday.

7. _____ Was eavesdropping on someone else's conversation.

8. _____ Begins at six o'clock every morning and lasts until noon.

9. _____ All of the evergreen trees.

B ▸ Practice

Here are more types of sentence fragments and ways to correct them.

3. When the fragment is a phrase with no subject or predicate, correct it by adding both a subject and a predicate. The original phrase may be part of either the subject or the predicate.

   Fragment: Along the Rio Grande.
   Correction: <u>The mule wandered</u> along the Rio Grande.

4. When the fragment is a phrase with only part of a verb, add a subject and complete the verb by adding a helping verb.

   Fragment: Hidden under the doormat.
   Complete sentence: <u>The spare key</u> is hidden under the doormat.

5. The fragment may be a subordinate clause. It will have both a subject and a predicate, but it will not make sense by itself. Subordinate clauses begin with words such as *after, although, as, because, if, since, though, unless, when, where,* and *while*. To correct a subordinate clause fragment, combine the fragment with a complete sentence.

   Fragment: Since he came back from England.
   Correction: Since he came back from England, <u>Rodney has been speaking with an accent</u>.

Correct each fragment by making it a complete sentence. If the item is a complete sentence, write *Correct* on the line.

1. Next to DiNardo's Pizza Parlor. _____

   _____

2. Raymond's coffee is cold. _____

   _____

3. Because her mother invited her. _____

   _____

4. Before the circus left town. _____

   _____

5. Both of the cars have rusted. _____

   _____

C ▸ Apply

Correct each of the sentence fragments below. Write the complete sentence on the line.

1. Ned and Samantha's favorite painting.

   _____

2. I'll start chopping the peppers. After you make the rice.

   _____

3. We stopped by the hardware store. To see our cousin.

   _____

4. Is open only on Tuesdays and Thursdays.

   _____

5. Jacques realized that he'd left his keys inside. As he was shutting the door.

   _____

6. The librarian and the police chief.

   _____

7. After she returned from Florida.

   _____

8. Knows how to pick a lock with a hairpin.

   _____

9. Old Bill the pirate. Gets sentimental when he smells the ocean.

   _____

10. I got lost outside of Chicago. Because I didn't have a map.

    _____

11. Hidden behind a painting of Napoleon.

    _____

12. Flying out of Los Angeles on Saturday.

    _____

D Check Up

For each item, choose the complete sentence.

1. **A** Went for a swim in the river.

   B A glittering swarm of dragonflies.

   C The canoe has a hole in the bottom.

   D In a clump of weeds on the riverbank.

2. **F** My high school home economics teacher.

   G Because she wants to know if she should quit her job.

   H Looked into her crystal ball.

   J Madame Zarah says that she can tell the future.

3. **A** Looking for an excuse to leave.

   B Drove all the way back to Tulsa.

   C Emma stopped for lunch in Boise.

   D The front right fender of the car.

4. **F** The singer saved her biggest hit for last.

   G A free concert in the park.

   H Behind the new pavilion.

   J Hoping to find an ice-cream stand.

Read the paragraph and look at the numbered, underlined parts. Choose the answer that is written correctly for each underlined part.

(5) The production of *The Real Thing* at the Heritage Theater. Was done entirely in sign language. The audience was composed of both hearing-impaired and hearing

(6) people. Sitting in total silence for two hours was an unusual experience. For the hearing playgoers. All who attended agreed that the play was a great success.

5. **A** The production of *The Real Thing* at the Heritage Theater was done entirely in sign language.

   B The production of *The Real Thing* at the Heritage Theater was done. Entirely in sign language.

   C The production of *The Real Thing*. At the Heritage Theater was done entirely. In sign language.

   D Correct as it is

6. **F** Sitting in total silence for two hours. Was an unusual experience. For the hearing playgoers.

   G Sitting in total silence for two hours was an unusual experience for the hearing playgoers.

   H Sitting in total silence. For two hours was an unusual experience for the hearing playgoers.

   J Correct as it is

Run-On Sentences

A **run-on sentence** is two or more sentences written as if they were one sentence. A run-on lacks the punctuation necessary to show where one idea ends and the next begins.

One type of run-on combines sentences and provides no punctuation between them, as in the example below. The first sentence is underlined.

<u>It is raining steadily now</u> it should stop soon.

Another kind of run-on combines sentences using just a comma. Such a run-on is often called a **comma splice**.

<u>It is raining steadily now</u>, it should stop soon.

Each of the run-on sentences below is really two sentences combined incorrectly. Underline the first sentence in each run-on.

1. The train is late, it should have been here at 4:30.

2. I don't know French does Henri speak any English?

3. The Regal Cinema closed down I used to go there every week.

4. Paula is leaving for Brazil on Tuesday, she's really excited.

5. Morrice is very athletic he wants to be a personal trainer.

6. Ian went to Boston, he has family there.

7. Ms. Glover was my supervisor now she works in Human Resources.

8. They don't have chocolate, would vanilla be okay?

Write *CS* beside each complete sentence and *RO* beside each run-on sentence.

9. _____ David lives in the suburbs it takes him over an hour to get to work.

10. _____ Noah plays the guitar and the mandolin.

11. _____ Both of Christina's dogs came from the pound when they were puppies.

12. _____ The plate is cracked maybe we can fix it.

13. _____ Angel was at the party, he's the tall one who always looks very serious.

B ▶ Practice

There are several ways to correct run-ons.

- Separate the sentences. Insert the correct end mark (period, exclamation point, question mark) after each sentence, and begin each sentence with a capital letter.

  The rain is falling steadily <u>now. It</u> should stop soon.

- Insert a comma after the first statement, and add a conjunction such as *and, but,* or *or* after the comma.

  The rain is falling steadily now<u>, but</u> it should stop soon.

- Insert a semicolon after the first statement. Do not capitalize the first word of the second statement.

  The rain is falling steadily now<u>; it</u> should stop soon.

- Insert a semicolon after the first statement. Then add a transition word such as *however, nevertheless,* or *therefore,* followed by a comma.

  The rain is falling steadily now<u>; however,</u> it should stop soon.

Correct each run-on sentence below. Write the corrected sentence on the line.

1. Frieda got a flashy new car, I saw it yesterday.

   _____

2. The yellow dress is on sale however it doesn't fit quite right.

   _____

3. The train conductor punched my ticket he put it above my seat.

   _____

4. Bryan paid with a twenty, the cashier forgot to give back his change.

   _____

5. Mary ordered lasagna, Joy asked for spaghetti with meatballs.

   _____

6. Be careful on Preston Road it's still under construction.

   _____

7. Knock on the door the buzzer is broken.

   _____

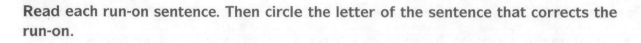

C ▸ Apply

Read each run-on sentence. Then circle the letter of the sentence that corrects the run-on.

1. There is plenty of cake left over would you like to take some home?
   - **A** There is plenty of cake left over. Would you like to take some home?
   - **B** There is plenty of cake left over, would you like to take some home?

2. Dr. Aziz likes baseball he enjoys the English game of cricket even more.
   - **A** Dr. Aziz likes baseball, he loves the English game of cricket even more.
   - **B** Dr. Aziz likes baseball, but he enjoys the English game of cricket even more.

3. These plants are dying do you think we should water them?
   - **A** These plants are dying. Do you think we should water them?
   - **B** These plants are dying, do you think we should water them?

4. Walter has always been afraid of heights he insists on climbing Bald Mountain.
   - **A** Walter has always been afraid of heights, he insists on climbing Bald Mountain.
   - **B** Walter has always been afraid of heights; however, he insists on climbing Bald Mountain.

5. Julie loves to run she'll race anyone who challenges her.
   - **A** Julie loves to run she'll race; anyone who challenges her.
   - **B** Julie loves to run; she'll race anyone who challenges her.

Identify the run-on sentences in the following paragraph. Then rewrite the paragraph correctly on the lines below.

The coffee house was filled with interesting people. A young couple sat by the window, they looked like they were arguing. A worried student had her books spread out in one of the booths she was reading and writing notes. An older man sat at a small table in the back, he kept looking up was he waiting for someone?

_____

_____

_____

_____

D Check Up

For each item, choose the complete sentence.

1. **A** The students played a joke on their teacher, she wasn't amused.

    B Jo loves to ride her bike; she hasn't driven a car in ten years.

    C Nancy's brother is here you should meet him.

    D Ten thousand birds nest; in the wetlands by the highway.

2. **F** I haven't read that book yet is it good?

    G Jan stopped by the neighbors' house she brought some cookies.

    H Carlos is a math whiz, he can solve any problem that you give him.

    J Dora and her cousin are fixing up an antique Ford.

3. **A** Anne loves jewelry her arms are covered in bracelets.

    B Hiro is very attached to his old T-shirt, he won't throw it out.

    C Mark has to move into a new place; his rent went up last month.

    D Dan thinks that the baseball players should strike however I don't agree.

4. **F** Bob and Claude went ice fishing; and had a great time.

    G I love the beach, but I don't like sand in my shoes.

    H Katherine can be really funny she'll make a great actress.

    J A grasshopper got into the living room, I brought it back outside.

Read the paragraph and look at the numbered, underlined parts. Choose the answer that is written correctly for each underlined part.

(5) The city of Montreal hosts many festivals, there is a festival for just about every theme. A few of Montreal's best-known events are the World-Film Festival,
(6) the Just for Laughs Festival, and the International Festival of Jazz. These festivals attract visitors from all over the world, and they are fun for Montreal's residents.

5. **A** The city of Montreal hosts many festivals there is, a festival for just about every theme.

    B The city of Montreal hosts many festivals there is a festival for just about every theme.

    C The city of Montreal hosts many festivals; there is a festival for just about every theme.

    D Correct as it is

6. **F** These festivals attract visitors from all over the world; and they are fun for Montreal's residents.

    G These festivals attract visitors from all over the world; however, they are fun for Montreal's residents.

    H These festivals attract visitors from all over the world, they are fun for Montreal's residents.

    J Correct as it is

Sentence Combining: Compound Sentence Parts

If all your sentences are about the same length, your writing can become monotonous. To give your writing variety, you may want to combine sentences or parts of sentences.

You can combine entire sentences to form a **compound sentence**. Each part, or **clause**, of a compound sentence has a subject and a predicate and can stand alone. Compound sentences are usually joined by the conjunctions *and, or, nor, but, yet,* or *for.*

> Pamela teaches science. She advises a science club.
> Pamela teaches science, and she advises a science club.
>   (independent clause)   (independent clause)

Often it is not necessary to use the entire second sentence. Look for common parts in the sentences that you want to combine, and use only the parts that are different. For example, look at the sample sentences above. Both subjects—*Pamela* and *she*—name the same person. You can combine the sentences in one simple sentence with a compound predicate.

> Pamela teaches science and advises a science club.

If two sentences with the same predicate are combined, the sentence that is formed has a compound subject.

> Abby was promoted. James was promoted.
> Abby and James were promoted.

In each item, underline the words that appear in both sentences. Then combine the two sentences by forming a compound part.

1. Ryan volunteers at the homeless shelter. Lisa volunteers at the homeless shelter.

   _____

2. Heather overslept. Heather was late for work.

   _____

3. A salad comes with every dinner. A vegetable comes with every dinner.

   _____

4. The icy roads made driving dangerous. The drifting snow made driving dangerous.

   _____

B Practice

Forming compound subjects and predicates is just one way to combine sentences with common parts. You can also combine sentences by forming other compound parts. Here are some examples:

> Rocky listens to jazz.
> Rocky listens to the blues.
> Rocky listens to jazz and the blues.

> This cafeteria serves Mexican food.
> This cafeteria serves American food.
> This cafeteria serves Mexican and American food.

Compare the first two sentences in each item. Underline the words that appear in both sentences. Then circle the letter of the sentence that correctly combines the sentences by forming a compound part.

1. The trip into the wilderness was difficult. The trip into the wilderness was dangerous.
   A The trip into the wilderness was difficult and the trip was dangerous.
   B The trip into the wilderness was difficult and dangerous.

2. Justin bought candy for his girlfriend. Justin bought flowers for his girlfriend.
   A Justin bought candy and flowers for his girlfriend.
   B Justin bought candy and Justin bought flowers for his girlfriend.

3. The couple invited many relatives to their wedding. The couple invited many friends to their wedding.
   A The couple invited many friends to their wedding and many relatives.
   B The couple invited many friends and relatives to their wedding.

4. I called your office. Your boss answered the phone.
   A I called your office, and your boss answered the phone.
   B I and your boss called your office and answered the phone.

5. The music shop rents instruments. The music shop sells instruments.
   A The music shop rents and sells instruments.
   B The music shop rents instruments and sells instruments, too.

6. Our store promises low prices. Our store promises friendly service.
   A Our store promises low prices and we promise friendly service.
   B Our store promises low prices and friendly service.

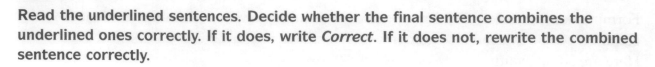

C Apply

Read the underlined sentences. Decide whether the final sentence combines the underlined ones correctly. If it does, write *Correct*. If it does not, rewrite the combined sentence correctly.

1. <u>I need to buy more film for my camera.</u>
    <u>I need to buy an extra battery for my camera.</u>
    I need to buy more film and I need an extra battery for my camera.

    _____

2. <u>I asked for iced tea.</u>
    <u>The waitress gave me coffee.</u>
    I asked for iced tea, so the waitress gave me coffee.

    _____

3. <u>Mr. Franklin collects rare coins.</u>
    <u>Mr. Franklin collects unusual coins.</u>
    The coins that Mr. Franklin collects are rare and they are unusual, too.

    _____

4. <u>The magician performed many fantastic tricks.</u>
    <u>He amazed the audience.</u>
    The magician performed many fantastic tricks and he amazed the audience.

    _____

5. <u>Add the chopped nuts to the cookie dough.</u>
    <u>Add the chocolate chips to the cookie dough.</u>
    Add the chopped nuts to the cookie dough and the chocolate chips.

    _____

6. <u>The salesman talked to many customers.</u>
    <u>Few of them placed orders.</u>
    The salesman talked to many customers, but few of them placed orders.

    _____

7. <u>The sports league presents awards every year.</u>
    <u>The sports league presents awards at a huge picnic.</u>
    <u>The sports league presents awards at a well-attended picnic.</u>
    The sports league presents awards every year at a huge picnic.

    _____

◆ D ▶ Check Up

Choose the sentence that best combines the underlined sentences.

1. <u>Joe went camping last summer.</u>
   <u>Louise went camping last summer.</u>

   A Joe and Louise went camping last summer.

   B Joe went and Louise went camping last summer.

   C Joe went camping last summer, and Louise went camping, too.

   D Joe and Louise, they went camping.

2. <u>Sean paints pictures with geometric shapes.</u>
   <u>Sean paints pictures with electric colors.</u>

   F Sean paints geometric, electric pictures.

   G Sean paints pictures with geometric, electric colors.

   H Sean paints pictures with geometric shapes and electric colors.

   J Sean paints pictures with shapes that are geometric and colors that are electric.

3. <u>Bernard rents a lot of videos.</u>
   <u>Bernard often forgets to return them on time.</u>

   A Bernard rents a lot of videos, and Bernard often forgets to return them on time.

   B Often, Bernard rents a lot of videos and often forgets to return them on time.

   C Bernard rents a lot of videos but often forgets to return them on time.

   D Bernard rents and forgets a lot of videos, returning them on time.

4. <u>The cat crept toward the bird.</u>
   <u>The cat crept slowly.</u>
   <u>The cat crept cautiously.</u>

   F Slow and cautious, the cat crept toward the bird.

   G The cat crept slowly toward the bird, and it crept cautiously.

   H The cat crept toward the bird, and it crept slowly and cautiously.

   J The cat crept slowly and cautiously toward the bird.

Sentence Combining: Subordinate Clauses

If you combine two sentences whose ideas are equally important, you form a compound sentence. Each clause in a compound sentence can stand alone as a complete sentence.

However, you may combine sentences where one idea is more important than the other, or you may wish to make one idea more important. In that case, you will form a complex sentence. A **complex sentence** contains an independent clause and a dependent clause. A **dependent clause** has a subject and a predicate, but it cannot stand alone as a sentence. Here are some examples:

The car <u>that I bought</u> is a lemon.

This dial indicates <u>how fast you are going</u>.

<u>While you were sleeping</u>, I rearranged all the furniture.

Read each sentence and look at the underlined clause. If the underlined clause is independent, write _IC_ on the line. If the underlined clause is a dependent clause, write _DC_.

1. The newspaper <u>that you are reading</u> is from last week. _____

2. <u>While Orson watched the movie</u>, he munched chips. _____

3. Some people want <u>whatever is popular at the moment</u>. _____

4. At craft fairs Olive priced her dolls competitively, and <u>she always sold out</u>. _____

5. Always save your work on a disk because you never know <u>when the computer may crash</u>. _____

6. Customers <u>who arrived at the store by 7:00 A.M.</u> received a free gift. _____

7. <u>The cookies were stale</u>, but we ate them anyway. _____

8. <u>Unless the rain stops soon</u>, the ballgame will be cancelled. _____

9. That old rolltop desk, <u>which belonged to my grandfather</u>, is very valuable. _____

10. The team played hard to the end <u>although they had no chance of winning</u>. _____

11. The table is new, but <u>I found the lamp in my parents' attic</u>. _____

12. Annie confessed <u>that she had always wanted to learn to yodel</u>. _____

B Practice

There may be more than one way to combine two or more sentences into a single complex sentence.

> Contestants ride boats. They have built the boats themselves.
> **(1)** Contestants ride boats <u>that they have built themselves</u>.
> **(2)** Contestants themselves have built the boats <u>that they ride</u>.

Both original sentences describe the boats. Therefore, either sentence can be used as the independent clause, and the other sentence can become a dependent clause. In the next example, the order of events is important.

> Rudi sanded the model plane. Then he painted the model.
> **(1)** <u>After Rudi sanded the model plane</u>, he painted it.
> **(2)** Rudi sanded the model plane <u>before he painted it</u>.

Here are some of the words often used when combining two sentences into a complex sentence: the pronouns *who, which, what, that, whoever, whatever*; the adverbs *how, when, where, why*; the conjunctions *after, although, as, because, before, if, since, so, unless, until*, and *while*.

For each item, circle the letter of the sentence that correctly combines the underlined sentences.

1. <u>The room was stuffy.</u>
   <u>Nancy opened all the windows.</u>

   A Because the room was stuffy, Nancy opened all the windows.

   B Because Nancy opened all the windows, the room was stuffy.

2. <u>We drove fifty miles into the desert.</u>
   <u>Then we discovered we were going in the wrong direction.</u>

   A We drove fifty miles into the desert after we discovered we were going in the wrong direction.

   B After we drove fifty miles into the desert, we discovered we were going in the wrong direction.

3. <u>Everyone in the library looked startled.</u>
   <u>I dropped a large dictionary on the floor.</u>

   A When everyone in the library looked startled, I dropped a large dictionary on the floor.

   B When I dropped a large dictionary on the floor, everyone in the library looked startled.

4. <u>Paul's suitcase was damaged.</u>
   <u>He lost some of the contents.</u>

   A Paul's suitcase was damaged, so he lost some of the contents.

   B Paul lost some of the contents of his suitcase, so his suitcase was damaged.

Read the underlined sentences. If the following complex sentence combines them correctly, write *Correct*. If it does not, write a correct complex sentence.

1. <u>Hernando enjoyed fishing in the cove.</u>
   <u>It was quiet and peaceful there.</u>

   Because Hernando enjoyed fishing in the cove, it was quiet and peaceful there.

   _____

2. <u>This afternoon I drove to Mindy's office.</u>
   <u>Her office is downtown.</u>

   This afternoon I drove to Mindy's office, which is downtown.

   _____

3. <u>My truck ran out of gas.</u>
   <u>I had to walk four miles to the nearest town.</u>

   My truck ran out of gas, after I had to walk four miles to the nearest town.

   _____

4. <u>Raymond neglected to level the ground properly.</u>
   <u>The patio stones are uneven.</u>

   Since the patio stones are uneven, Raymond neglected to level the ground properly.

   _____

5. <u>We must leave right now.</u>
   <u>Otherwise, I will be late.</u>

   We must leave right now unless I will be late.

   _____

6. <u>Jacqueline received a transfer.</u>
   <u>She had requested the transfer.</u>

   Jacqueline received the transfer that she had requested.

   _____

D Check Up

Read the underlined sentences. Choose the compound or complex sentence that correctly combines the underlined sentences.

1. The factory received more orders.
   Everyone is working overtime.

   A The factory received more orders unless everyone is working overtime.

   B Everyone is working overtime, but the factory received more orders.

   C The factory received more orders, so everyone is working overtime.

   D Everyone in the factory has been ordered to work overtime.

2. The weather report called for freezing temperatures.
   Caleb wore his heavy coat and hat.

   F The weather report called for freezing temperatures, but Caleb wore his heavy coat and hat.

   G Caleb wore his heavy coat and hat because the weather report called for freezing temperatures.

   H Although Caleb wore his heavy coat and hat, the weather report called for freezing temperatures.

   J The weather report called for freezing temperatures, or Caleb wore his heavy coat and hat.

3. The bus company requires exact fares.
   I have only a five dollar bill.

   A Since I have only a five dollar bill, the bus company requires exact fares.

   B Although I have only a five dollar bill, the bus company requires exact fares.

   C The bus company requires exact fares, or I have only a five dollar bill.

   D The bus company requires exact fares, but I have only a five dollar bill.

4. Bethany usually parks in the underground garage.
   It is close to her office.

   F Bethany usually parks in the underground garage while it is close to her office.

   G Because Bethany usually parks in the underground garage, it is close to her office.

   H Whenever the underground garage is close to her office, Bethany parks in it.

   J Bethany usually parks in the underground garage that is close to her office.

A ▶ Introduce

Sentence Combining: Adding Modifiers

To make your writing more interesting, use adjective and adjective details about persons, places, and things. You may find yourself writing short sentences with a separate detail in each. Combine these sentences in a single, more interesting sentence.

Adjectives tell *which one, what kind,* or *how many* about a noun or pronoun. When you move an adjective from one sentence into another, place it before the word it modifies. Place an adjective phrase after the word it modifies.

Adding an adjective:

Vinnie bought a couch on sale.
The couch was <u>leather</u>.

Vinnie bought a <u>leather</u> couch on sale.

Adding an adjective phrase:

Those peaches are ripe and juicy.
The peaches are <u>in the orchard</u>.

Those peaches <u>in the orchard</u> are ripe and juicy.

Read each pair of sentences. In the second sentence, underline the noun that is modified. Underline the same noun in the first sentence. Then combine the sentences, adding the modifier to the first sentence.

1. We always rent a cabin for the summer. The cabin is near the Smoky Mountains.

   _____

2. One entry in the art exhibit stood out from the rest. The entry was ornate.

   _____

3. My cat keeps her kittens in a basket. The basket is under the porch.

   _____

4. During the play-offs, only a few seats were empty. The seats were in the upper deck.

   _____

5. The water from the spring is cool and refreshing. The spring is underground.

   _____

B ▸ Practice

Adverbs and adverb phrases usually modify verbs. They tell *how, when, where,* or *why* an action happens. They may also modify adjectives and other adverbs. In general, try to place modifiers close to the words they modify. However, adverbs that modify verbs usually make sense in different parts of the sentence.

Adding an adverb:

Damon repaired the clock.
He worked <u>carefully</u>.

Damon carefully repaired the clock. *or*
Damon repaired the clock carefully. *or*
Carefully, Damon repaired the clock.

Each sentence in Column B is a combination of one of the sentence pairs in Column A. On the line in Column A, write the letter of the matching sentence from Column B.

1. The children toiled over the puzzle.

   They worked patiently. _____

2. Bill shops at the home improvement store. He shops there frequently.

   _____

3. We planted new shrubs and flowers.

   We did this around the patio. _____

4. Marc's car stalled in traffic. It stalled during rush hour. _____

5. New tenants leased the empty apartment. It happened recently.

   _____

A   Bill frequently shops at the home improvement store.

B   Marc's car stalled in traffic during rush hour.

C   The children toiled patiently over the puzzle.

D   New tenants recently leased the empty apartment.

E   We planted new shrubs and flowers around the patio.

For each item, combine the sentences. Be sure not to lose any modifiers.

6. Two linemen lunged at the loose football. They lunged frantically.

   _____

7. Our cruise ship stopped in San Juan. It stopped for three days.

   _____

C Apply

Read each set of underlined sentences. Decide whether the final sentence combines the underlined ones correctly. If it does, write *Correct*. If it does not, rewrite the combined sentence correctly.

1. Sophia reconstructed the broken vase.
   She worked slowly. She worked carefully.
   Sophia reconstructed the broken vase, and she did it slowly and carefully, too.

   _____

2. The magician appeared to walk through a wall.
   The wall was stone.
   The magician appeared to walk through a wall, and it was stone.

   _____

3. The bugler played "Taps" at the ceremony.
   He played reverently.
   The bugler reverently played "Taps" at the ceremony.

   _____

4. As a consultant, Mr. Getz traveled extensively.
   He traveled all over the world.
   As a consultant, Mr. Getz traveled extensively and traveled all over the world.

   _____

5. At the Apple Butter Festival, the aroma of cooked apples filled the air.
   The aroma was sweet. The air was hazy.
   At the Apple Butter Festival, the sweet aroma of cooked apples filled the hazy air.

   _____

6. We stopped for coffee.
   We stopped after the movie.
   We stopped for coffee, and we did it after the movie.

   _____

7. The skier sped down the steep slope.
   The skier skied smoothly. The skier moved gracefully.
   The skier smoothly sped down the steep slope and gracefully, too.

   _____

Read the underlined sentences. Then choose the sentence that best combines the underlined sentences.

1. <u>Maurice hobbled on the crutches.</u>
   <u>He moved awkwardly.</u>

   A Maurice hobbled on the crutches, and he hobbled awkwardly.

   B Maurice awkwardly hobbled on the crutches.

   C Maurice hobbled on the awkward crutches.

   D Maurice, who moved awkwardly on the crutches, hobbled on the crutches.

2. <u>Lambs frolicked in the green pasture.</u>
   <u>There were three lambs.</u>
   <u>They frolicked playfully.</u>

   F Three lambs playfully frolicked in the green pasture.

   G Lambs frolicked playfully in the green pasture, and there were three of them.

   H Three lambs frolicked in the green pasture, and they frolicked playfully.

   J Three frolicsome and playful lambs were in the green pasture.

3. <u>Lucia stenciled a border of ivy leaves.</u>
   <u>She stenciled on the dining room wall.</u>

   A On the dining room wall is a border, and Lucia stenciled ivy leaves on it.

   B Lucia stenciled a border of ivy leaves, and she put them on the dining room wall.

   C Lucia stenciled on the dining room wall, and she put a border of ivy leaves on it.

   D Lucia stenciled a border of ivy leaves on the dining room wall.

4. <u>The entire workforce waited for the inspectors to arrive.</u>
   <u>They waited nervously.</u>

   F The entire workforce waited for the inspectors to arrive nervously.

   G The entire workforce waited for the inspectors to arrive, and they waited nervously.

   H The entire workforce waited nervously for the inspectors to arrive.

   J The entire workforce waited for the inspectors nervously to arrive.

Sentence Clarity: Misplaced Modifiers

When you add a modifying phrase to a sentence, be sure to place it where it makes sense. Any modifier describing a noun or a pronoun belongs just before or just after the word it describes. A modifier placed in the wrong part of a sentence often leads to confusion. Note how, in the first sentence below, misplacing the underlined phrase results in a wrong message.

Misplaced: The pudding is for you <u>in the yellow bowl</u>.

Correct: The pudding <u>in the yellow bowl</u> is for you.

In the first sentence, the modifier is closer to *you* than it is to *pudding*. Therefore, the sentence suggests that the person spoken to is in the yellow bowl. The second sentence makes it clear that it is the pudding that is in the bowl.

A **misplaced modifier** is any modifier that is placed in a sentence in such a way that it describes the wrong person or thing. You can usually avoid misplaced modifiers by placing every descriptive phrase as close as possible to the word it modifies.

Find the misplaced modifier in each sentence. Then rewrite the sentence, correcting the position of the modifier.

1. Any customer can order a dining room set with a good credit rating.

   _____

2. Hiding acorns under a bush, I saw a brown squirrel.

   _____

3. Several coins rolled into the street that fell from Zubin's pocket.

   _____

4. The pencils are sharp in that box, but they have no erasers.

   _____

5. Marooned on a desert island, the story is about a pirate.

   _____

6. Our neighbors' dog irritates us, always barking.

   _____

B Practice

A modifying phrase can cause confusion when it is added to a sentence that has no word for it to modify. Here is an example:

> Crossing the ocean, the weather was awful.

There is no word in the sentence modified by the phrase *crossing the ocean*. Such a phrase, which is not connected to any word in its sentence, is called a **dangling modifier**. Be sure that when you add a modifier to a sentence, the modifier relates to a specific word in the sentence. Correct a sentence with a dangling modifier by rewriting it to include the word that is modified.

> Crossing the ocean, the travelers experienced awful weather.

For each item, circle the letter of the sentence that is written correctly without any dangling modifiers.

1. A With steady income from investments, retirement can be pleasant.
   B With steady income from investments, a person can enjoy retirement.

2. A Falling on the slick ice, you could break a bone.
   B Falling on the slick ice, broken bones are a possibility.

3. A Perry came home to a fine dinner by the turnpike.
   B After traveling on the turnpike, Perry came home to a fine dinner.

4. A Listening to the radio, we heard some old favorites.
   B Listening to the radio, the beat of the drums was strong and steady.

5. A Covered with chocolate, the calories in that sundae must be high!
   B When you are trying to lose weight, choosing a sundae is a bad idea.

6. A With two scoops, Moira is eating a chocolate ice-cream cone.
   B Moira is eating a chocolate ice-cream cone with two scoops.

7. A Joel found the CD he lost last summer recently.
   B Joel recently found the CD he lost last summer.

8. A Searching in the mountains of Siberia, an archeologist found a major treasure.
   B The Russian archeologist discovered a 2400-year-old mummy searching in the mountains of Siberia.

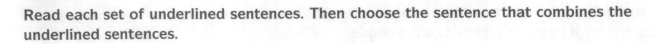

C ▸ Apply

Read each set of underlined sentences. Then choose the sentence that combines the underlined sentences.

1. <u>Alice was swimming at a hotel pool.</u>
   <u>A toddler fell into the water.</u>
   <u>Alice saved the child.</u>

   A Swimming at a hotel pool, a toddler fell into the water, and Alice saved the child.

   B Alice, swimming at a hotel pool, saved a toddler who fell into the water.

   C Swimming at a hotel pool, a toddler who fell into the water was saved.

2. <u>Let the dough rise for about an hour.</u>
   <u>Then divide it into four equal portions.</u>

   F After rising for about an hour, divide the dough into four equal portions.

   G For about an hour, divide the dough which has risen into four equal portions.

   H After letting the dough rise for about an hour, divide it into four equal portions.

3. <u>Tippy was originally named Tabitha.</u>
   <u>She got her nickname from a little brother.</u>
   <u>Her brother couldn't say her name.</u>

   A Originally named Tabitha, Tippy got her nickname from a little brother who couldn't say her name.

   B Originally named Tabitha, her nickname Tippy came from a little brother who couldn't say her name.

   C Originally named Tabitha, a little brother who couldn't say her name gave Tippy her nickname.

Read the underlined sentences. If the final sentence combines the underlined ones correctly, write *Correct*. If it does not, rewrite the combined sentence correctly.

4. <u>Allen was cutting the lawn.</u>
   <u>A skunk crossed the lawn in front of him.</u>
   Cutting the lawn, a skunk crossed the lawn in front of Allen.

   _____

5. <u>Ilona's cell phone was lying in her pocket.</u>
   <u>It rang during an orchestra concert.</u>
   Ilona's cell phone rang during an orchestra concert lying in her pocket.

   _____

For each item, choose the sentence that has no misplaced or dangling modifiers.

1. **A** Shooting across the night sky, we saw a meteor.

    B My nephew impressed everyone playing a cornet solo at the high school band concert.

    C Buildings on the east side of the city were not damaged by the tornado.

    D After stopping at a gas station on the way here, my tank is full.

2. **F** Most of the parents at the PTA meeting voted to hold a fundraiser.

    G Laying off many workers at area plants, citizens have seen the local economy falter.

    H With a malfunctioning timer, no one can use this microwave oven.

    J Several neighbors tried out for parts in a play about a vampire that I know.

3. **A** First enjoyed by Native Americans, we prepare succotash by cooking lima beans and corn together.

    B The knocker on the front door makes a sound heard throughout the entire house.

    C Despite record cold temperatures, fans camped out overnight for tickets dropping into the 30s Fahrenheit.

    D Returning from the sea, relieved families greeted the crews of the fishing vessels.

4. **F** Lydia accidentally left the album on the train filled with family photographs.

    G Before deciding whom to vote for, a review of the candidates' records is recommended.

    H With delicate pink flowers, Evan planted rhododendrons along the north edge of the yard.

    J Carrying a bulky desk down the stairs, the movers scraped paint off the walls.

5. **A** Holding little Fritz up to the mirror, the baby reached toward his reflection.

    B The clothes that Indira put into the washer with her new red towels came out pink.

    C Not long after surgery, Enrique greeted visitors at the hospital on his elbow.

    D Elected the second president of the United States, ancestors of John Adams had settled in Massachusetts before 1640.

6. **F** Yelling enthusiastically, the arena was a noisy bedlam.

    G Eliza carved two jack-o'-lanterns for her children with triangle eyes and oval mouths.

    H Speaking at Monday's City Council meeting, Leonard asked for improved street lighting.

    J Spread with jam, almost every child likes toast.

Sentence Clarity: Parallel Structure

You find **parallel structure** in a sentence with two elements that are used in the same way and are the same part of speech. For example, both examples below show parallel structure. Each sentence has a compound subject, and both parts of the subject are the same part of speech.

> **Parallel:** A <u>pitcher</u> and a <u>catcher</u> are both necessary for a baseball game. (compound subject; both parts of the subject are nouns)

> **Parallel:** <u>To pitch</u> and <u>to catch</u> require different talents. (compound subject; both parts of the subject begin with *to*)

A sentence has **nonparallel structure** when it uses two different types of words, phrases, or clauses to serve the same purpose.

> **Nonparallel:** <u>The skills of a good pitcher</u> and <u>to catch well</u> are both desirable. (a noun phrase and a phrase beginning with *to* are used as subjects)

Use parallel structure in compound parts of all types. Mixing unlike, nonparallel elements makes it difficult for listeners or readers to recognize which parts of a sentence are working together.

In each sentence, two words or phrases used for the same purpose are underlined. Decide whether the underlined elements show parallel structure or nonparallel structure.

1. Della enjoys <u>making new friends</u> and <u>seeing old ones</u>.

   A parallel structure

   B nonparallel structure

2. Voters approved <u>a new tax</u> and <u>that the city could build a new city hall</u>.

   A parallel structure

   B nonparallel structure

3. Every October, <u>buying pumpkins</u> and <u>carving jack-o'-lanterns</u> are popular family activities.

   A parallel structure

   B nonparallel structure

4. <u>Marriage</u> and <u>to start a new job</u> can both be frightening experiences.

   A parallel structure

   B nonparallel structure

5. <u>Crying</u> and <u>to sleep</u> are two of the things my toddler does best.

   A parallel structure

   B nonparallel structure

6. <u>Practicing defense</u> and <u>building endurance</u> has helped the team's record.

   A parallel structure

   B nonparallel structure

B Practice

An **infinitive** is a verb in its present tense form preceded by the word *to*. Infinitives and infinitive phrases are often used as nouns.

The candidate expected <u>to win by a landslide</u> and <u>to take office quickly</u>.

A **gerund** is a verb in its present tense form that ends in *-ing*. It is always used as a noun.

<u>Negotiating intelligently</u> and <u>creating good partnerships</u> are the two skills that make John a successful businessman.

Parallel structure also applies to infinitives and gerunds.

Parallel: Guests may choose <u>to rise early</u> or <u>to sleep late</u>.
<u>Rising early</u> or <u>sleeping late</u> are two options for guests.

Nonparallel: <u>Sanding the wood</u> and <u>to stain it</u> are the next steps.

Read each sentence, paying special attention to the underlined part. Choose the answer that is parallel to the underlined sentence part.

1. The sales assistant's job is <u>to maintain inventory</u> and _____.

   A filing periodic reports

   B to file periodic reports

   C she also files reports

   D will file periodic reports

2. My cousin was busy <u>cooking</u> dinner and _____ the baby's diaper.

   F to change

   G the change of

   H changes

   J changing

3. <u>Cutting the grass</u> and _____ are Dad's least favorite jobs.

   A clipping the hedges

   B to clip the hedges

   C clips the hedges

   D clipped the hedges

4. Before he retired, Jake was <u>operating a gas station</u> and _____.

   F selling plants

   G to sell plants

   H sold plants

   J sells plants

5. <u>Filling the gas tank</u> and _____ cleaned out my wallet.

   A paying my library fine

   B paid my library fine

   C to pay my library fine

   D when I was paying my library fine

6. As a mother, Maria believes that her most important duties are <u>to keep her children safe</u> and _____.

   F give them a good education

   G to give them a good education

   H giving them a good education

   J gave them a good education

Choose the answer that is written correctly for the underlined part.

1. Gerry bought a computer to play online games and <u>for sending e-mail</u>.

   A   for when she wants to send e-mail

   B   to send e-mail

   C   she can send e-mail

   D   Correct as it is

2. Checking the wiring, cleaning the ducts, and <u>replace</u> the filter are the repairman's duties.

   F   replaced

   G   replacing

   H   replaces

   J   Correct as it is

3. During this past season, Woodie's problems included injuries, a batting slump, and <u>when he had a disagreement</u> with the manager.

   A   when he disagreed

   B   to disagree

   C   a disagreement

   D   Correct as it is

4. Are you guilty of cheating at solitaire or <u>lying</u> about your weight?

   F   to lie

   G   lie

   H   have lied

   J   Correct as it is

5. Carrying the dishes to the sink and <u>to put them</u> into the dishwasher will take just a few minutes.

   A   put them

   B   putting them

   C   when we put them

   D   Correct as it is

6. Being prompt and <u>dresses well</u> are two things that help you to make a good first impression.

   F   to dress well

   G   dressing well

   H   dress well

   J   Correct as it is

7. Is feng shui concerned with finding the right spot for one's home or <u>how to decide</u> where to place the furniture?

   A   deciding

   B   to decide

   C   decisions about

   D   Correct as it is

8. Over the weekend the staff was tagging all the old merchandise, moving it to the clearance shelves, and <u>we put out</u> the new displays and stock.

   F   they put out

   G   had put out

   H   putting out

   J   Correct as it is

Read the passage and look at the numbered, underlined parts. Choose the answer that is written correctly for each underlined part. Be sure that each sentence with compound parts has parallel structure.

During a single year, an active theater might present six or more plays. Props, or properties, may be needed for scenes in which swords are swung, people hide
(1) in rolltop desks, and <u>exploding chickens</u>. Who finds all these things for the stage manager? The propmaster does.

A successful propmaster needs a good memory, a good imagination,
(2) and <u>good relationships</u> with propmasters at other theaters. He or she depends on
(3) memory and <u>if they list all the props</u> the theater owns to find just the right prop amid the thousands of props in storage. Imagination comes in handy when
(4) a show requires something <u>new and strangely</u>. It's up to the propmaster to
(5) design whatever is needed and then <u>goes out and finds</u> the materials for it. When all else fails, a propmaster might need a little help from his or her friends. If so, it's nice if those friends are propmasters at other theaters, with
(6) <u>the storerooms that they have themselves and being creative</u>.

1. **A** chickens explode

    B to explode chickens

    C chickens that explode

    D Correct as it is

2. **F** to relate well with

    G relating well with

    H relates well with

    J Correct as it is

3. **A** a list of all the props

    B listing all the props

    C to list all the props

    D Correct as it is

4. **F** newly and strange

    G newly and strangely

    H new and strange

    J Correct as it is

5. **A** to go out and finding

    B going out and find

    C to go out and find

    D Correct as it is

6. **F** their own storerooms and creativity

    G their own storerooms and they're creative

    H their own storerooms and to be creative

    J Correct as it is

A ▸ Introduce

Sentence Clarity: Verbosity and Repetition

Writing that is **verbose** is unnecessarily wordy. Sentences may be padded by empty words and phrases such as *really, very,* and *to tell the truth.* The same idea may be repeated, perhaps in different words, but without new details. In these examples, notice how the extra words do not strengthen the message but, instead, make the sentences tiresome.

Verbose: During the month of June, Rudy was ill and not well at all at that particular point in time.

Concise: During June, Rudy was ill.

Verbose: Not a single person of my acquaintance that I know has any talent or ability or even experience in playing the harp.

Concise: Nobody I know plays the harp.

Read each pair of sentences. Circle the letter of the sentence that is concise.

1. **A** Kim was exhausted and so tired that he went home during the hour he had for lunch so he could lie down and take a nap on his bed there.

    B Exhausted, Kim went home during his lunch hour for a nap.

2. **A** Most of the movie critics said that *Mousepad* was too long.

    B Most of the critics who review movies said that, in their opinion, the movie named *Mousepad* was too long and had way too many scenes and scenes that went on and on.

3. **A** Amaryllis has never liked her name, not a bit, because she thinks it sounds old-fashioned and not modern, so she has always disliked the name.

    B Amaryllis has never liked her name because it sounds old-fashioned to her.

4. **A** On the whole, the prices at Discount Marketplace are usually lower than what they ask for at Massive Foods, but, of course, that's not true in some cases that are exceptions.

    B Usually, prices at Discount Marketplace are lower than prices at Massive Foods.

5. **A** Edna exercises daily before going to work.

    B Everyday before she goes to work, Edna exercises when she gets up in the morning.

Read each verbose sentence below and the three pairs of words or phrases from the sentence. Choose the answer with pairs that <u>do not</u> say the same thing.

1. If you want my opinion, I think that the taste of decaf coffee is superior and better than that of regular coffee.

   A If you want my opinion/I think

   B If you want my opinion/the taste of decaf coffee

   C superior/better than

2. While you're getting ready for work tomorrow morning, before you leave the house for the office, call me early in the day.

   F While you're getting ready for work/before you leave the house for the office

   G tomorrow morning/early in the day

   H before you leave the house for the office/call me

3. The beautiful heroine, who is the most important character in the story, is both smart and very attractive.

   A beautiful/smart

   B beautiful/very attractive

   C heroine/character in the story

4. War veterans who return home after serving in conflict are often changed by their experiences and everything they went through.

   F War veterans/after serving in conflict

   G War veterans/are often changed

   H their experiences/everything they went through

Read the sentence. Then choose the answer that lists words or phrases that <u>cannot</u> be dropped from the sentence without losing some of the meaning.

5. When I listen to my favorite radio station that I usually turn to, I like the music that I hear the station playing.

   A that I usually turn to

   B I like the music

   C that I hear the station playing

6. Kosta's Maid Service will be happy and delighted to save you from dull, boring jobs by doing the dirty work around your house.

   F Kosta's Maid Service

   G and delighted

   H boring

C Apply

Read each sentence and look at its underlined part. Choose the answer that is written correctly for the underlined part.

1. <u>In most cases, the typical response</u> of the bargain hunter to a "Clearance" sign is immediate curiosity.

   A Usually, in most cases, the typical response

   B The typical response

   C A response

   D Correct as it is

2. Even a skillful reader may need to reread <u>a difficult passage</u>.

   F a really difficult passage

   G a passage that is difficult and hard to make sense of

   H a difficult, hard-to-understand passage

   J Correct as it is

3. The <u>heavy, wet rain overflowed</u> the gutter above the store exit, drenching customers as they left.

   A heavy, wet rain filled

   B wet rain overflowed

   C heavy rain overflowed

   D Correct as it is

4. The recycling facility accepts glass, aluminum cans, and <u>products that are made of paper and cardboard</u>.

   F paper and cardboard products

   G paper products and cardboard products

   H products that are paper and cardboard

   J Correct as it is

Rewrite each of the following verbose sentences, dropping unnecessary words and phrases. Be careful not to change the meaning of the sentences.

5. Most of these types of problems could definitely be avoided with traffic signs that are placed correctly.

   _____

6. The guest on the late-night show who was a comedian delivered a boring, repetitive monologue, saying the same dull and tiresome jokes over and over.

   _____

7. Carmakers bring out new vehicles every year, and their purpose is to tempt people who already own cars to move up to the most recent, latest models.

   _____

For each item, choose the sentence that is written correctly and concisely.

1. **A** Mitzy loves to work in the garden until the days get cold and dreary, the temperature falls, and the skies are cloudy all day long.

   B Lars, scare those rabbits away from the vegetables and the lettuce immediately right away!

   C After being a member of the garden club in her suburb for twelve years, she is now the president of the group.

   D There are, most likely, many reasons why a person chooses a hobby, but probably one of the big reasons why some people like gardening is that those people just like being outside.

2. **F** After an hour or so in the lobby of the bus station, where they could do nothing but sit, the children became unruly and hard to control.

   G Are you waiting to board a bus, or are you here to pick up arrivals?

   H Tickets for the bus are definitely cheaper than the more expensive tickets for a plane.

   J People who were on the very late bus that arrived three hours after the scheduled time were really hungry and famished when they finally got off the bus.

3. **A** The weather last Saturday was excellent, so the high school graduation ceremonies were held outside.

   B At the commencement, the person giving the commencement address, who happened to be the mayor, kept everyone's attention.

   C Diplomas were awarded to a record number of students, members of the largest class graduating from the school to date.

   D Even before the end of the planned formalities, many guests who were sitting in the stands left their seats while the ceremony was still going on.

4. **F** Some documentaries about history that you can see on the educational TV stations are really fascinating.

   G In the near future, coming on tonight is a show about the Civil War and its effects.

   H Naturally, as you'd expect, a good deal of the program discusses the background of slavery in the South, talking about how the South came to depend on the so-called free labor of slaves.

   J Although the Emancipation Proclamation was a great step forward, it covered only those areas under Union control.

Complete Sentences, Fragments, and Run-Ons

Every complete sentence has a **subject** and a **predicate**. The subject names the person or thing that is doing something. The predicate tells what the subject is doing. It always includes a verb.

A **fragment** lacks at least one of these parts, while a **run-on sentence** combines two or more sentences without adequate punctuation. Find and fill in missing sentence parts. Punctuate and capitalize correctly.

Sentence Combining

Combine sentences that tell about the same topic by forming **compound sentences** or simple sentences with compound sentence parts.

> Geese fly <u>south in fall</u>. Geese fly <u>north in spring</u>.
> Geese fly <u>south in fall and north in spring</u>.

You can also combine whole sentences to form **complex sentences**. Both clauses in a compound sentence can stand alone. In a complex sentence, only one of the clauses is able to stand alone.

> The news program goes off at 11:30 P.M. Then we go to bed.
> When the news program goes off at 11:30 P.M., we go to bed.

You can move modifiers from one sentence to another that tells about the same object or action. Be sure to position the modifiers correctly.

Sentence Clarity

A modifier placed so that it describes the wrong word is called a **misplaced modifier**. If there is no word in the sentence for a modifier to describe, it is a **dangling modifier**. Revise sentences with misplaced or dangling modifiers to create sentences that make sense.

> **Misplaced:** The woman used a cell phone <u>in the red swimsuit</u>.
> **Correct:** The woman <u>in the red swimsuit</u> used a cell phone.

A sentence with parallel structure has words or phrases that are used in the same way and are the same part of speech.

> **Nonparallel:** Leslie avoids <u>criticizing</u> others and <u>to help</u> them.
> **Parallel:** Leslie avoids <u>criticizing</u> others and <u>helping</u> them.

Writing that uses many words to say very little is **verbose**. Try to be concise in your writing, avoiding empty words and repetition.

For each item, choose the sentence that is written correctly, with correct capitalization and punctuation. Be sure the sentence you choose is complete, makes sense, uses parallel structure, and avoids verbosity.

1. **A** A reporter on the news said in her report that it has been announced that the mayor will speak today.

    B The mayor will be at the community college, a new department is being opened.

    C The mayor himself is a graduate of the college.

    D Before he joined Peace Corps and then earned a degree in law.

2. **F** Aiming to become a famous chef, fame is already coming to Andrew.

    G Local food critics in this area call the restaurant where he works one of the best in our town.

    H He is noted for using exotic ingredients and to make unexpected combinations.

    J Andrew plans to open his own restaurant soon.

3. **A** The garage needs a coat of paint.

    B Not the worst problem with the building.

    C The roof leaks, the floor is cracked.

    D More often than not, the door usually doesn't open all the way most of the time.

4. **F** While the guests at the wedding reception were going through the receiving line.

    G The best man is the groom's older brother, Peter.

    H Have you seen the beautiful wedding cake, it looks delicious.

    J On their honeymoon, the couple will take a cruise and lying on a beach in the Caribbean.

5. **A** Choosing a name for a baby, not an easy task.

    B Some boys are named Marion it sounds like Marian.

    C Some names, such as Hilary, are given to both boys and girls.

    D Giving children unusual names is risky, for many children don't always like being different.

6. **F** People with shady gardens shouldn't buy sun-loving plants that don't like shade.

    G Consider hostas, which thrive in shady areas.

    H It's important to prepare the soil well and watering transplants regularly for the first week.

    J With at least a few hours of sunlight in the morning.

Read each set of underlined sentences. Choose the sentence that correctly combines the underlined sentences.

7. Joshua went to the museum to see dinosaurs.
   Joshua's mother went to the museum to see dinosaurs.

   A Joshua went to the museum to see dinosaurs, and so did his mother.

   B Joshua and his mother went to the museum to see dinosaurs.

   C When Joshua went to the museum to see dinosaurs, his mother went, too.

   D Joshua and his mother and dinosaurs were at the museum.

8. Cheese is part of many popular dishes.
   Cheese is made from soured milk.

   F Cheese is part of many popular dishes, and it's made from soured milk.

   G Because cheese is made from soured milk, it is part of many popular dishes.

   H Cheese, which is made from soured milk, is part of many popular dishes.

   J Cheese is part of many popular dishes made from soured milk.

9. The model home has a spacious kitchen.
   The kitchen has a marble countertop.

   A The model home has a spacious kitchen, or the kitchen has a marble countertop.

   B The model home, whose kitchen is spacious, has a marble countertop.

   C The model home has a spacious kitchen with a marble countertop.

   D Although the model home has a spacious kitchen, it also has a marble countertop.

10. Two motorcycles raced on a track.
    They moved recklessly.
    The track was in an oval shape.

    F Two motorcycles raced recklessly on an oval track.

    G In an oval shape, two motorcycles raced recklessly on a track.

    H Two motorcycles that moved recklessly raced on a track that was oval.

    J Two motorcycles raced on a track recklessly in an oval shape.

The following is the greeting and body of a letter. Look at its numbered, underlined parts. Choose the answers below that are written correctly for each underlined part.

Dear Mr. Hughes,

   I have a question about a photo in your latest book. I hope you can help me.

(11) The photo is of immigrants on page 43 at Ellis Island. I believe that there's a good

(12) chance that probably the man and woman in the photo may be my grandparents, who died almost twenty years ago. We have old photos of my grandparents,

(13) the photos were taken shortly after they arrived in the United States. The couple in

(14) your picture look very similar. Something else is even more important. That is that the woman in your photo is wearing a shawl that matches the one my

(15) grandmother left me. Can you send me information about the photo and telling me how to get a copy?

(16)   Thank you for your help and for the fine book, which I enjoyed very much.

11. **A** The photo is of immigrants on page 43 who are at Ellis Island.

    B The photo is of immigrants at Ellis Island on page 43.

    C The photo on page 43 is of immigrants at Ellis Island.

    D Correct as it is

12. **F** the man and woman in the photo

    G probably the man and woman in the photo

    H without a doubt the man and woman in the photo

    J Correct as it is

13. **A** although the photos were taken

    B taken

    C or the photos were taken

    D Correct as it is

14. **F** What is even more important is that the woman

    G Something else is even more important than the woman,

    H Something else! The woman

    J Correct as it is

15. **A** send me information about the photo. Telling me

    B sending me information about the photo and telling me

    C send me information about the photo and tell me

    D Correct as it is

16. **F** help and for the fine book, I enjoyed it very much.

    G help, which I enjoyed very much, and for the fine book.

    H help and for the fine book. Which I enjoyed it very much.

    J Correct as it is

The Main Idea of a Paragraph

To form a paragraph, a writer groups several sentences together. These sentences work together to support a single idea, called the **main idea.** Often, one sentence states the main idea of the paragraph. This sentence is the **topic sentence** of the paragraph.

The topic sentence is underlined in the following paragraph.

> <u>Harriet Tubman is one of the bravest characters in all of American history</u>. She was raised in slavery in the U.S. South and escaped in 1849 at the age of 29. Instead of hiding quietly in the North, she became a conductor on the Underground Railroad. She returned to the dangerous South nineteen times to help other slaves escape. Over the years, she guided three hundred people to their freedom. Although large rewards were offered for her capture, Tubman was never caught. She even went on to serve the U.S. army as a spy during the Civil War.

The topic sentence stated the main idea of the paragraph. Readers could expect that the paragraph would give details about Harriet Tubman and examples of her bravery.

For each paragraph, choose the main idea and underline the topic sentence.

1. Gloria really knows how to travel light. For a three-week vacation, she packs only a few tops, two pairs of pants, and a skirt. Each of the tops can be worn with any of the bottoms. If she goes out dancing or eats at a nice restaurant, she simply adds jewelry to dress her outfit up. Her friends with heavy luggage envy her when she waltzes out of the airport with just a small carry-on bag.

    A Jewelry can dress up a plain outfit.

    B People with heavy luggage envy Gloria.

    C Gloria packs light when she travels.

2. The Spamarama, held each May in Austin, Texas, is an occasion for many unusual contests. One contest, the Spam Toss, allows participants to show off their athletic abilities by throwing a hunk of Spam as far as they can. Another contest, the Spam-Eating Contest, is just what is sounds like. It is recommended that contestants arrive very hungry. Perhaps the most exciting contest is the Pork Pull. Two teams compete in a tug-of-war, trying to drag each other into a pool of Spam jelly.

    F The Pork Pull is the most exciting contest held in Austin, Texas.

    G The Spamarama is made up of several unusual contests.

    H Contestants who wish to compete at the Spamarama should arrive very hungry.

B Practice

Read each paragraph below. Choose its topic sentence from among the four lettered sentences. Write the letter of the topic sentence on the blank line.

A   Austin became the capital of Texas because of the determination of Mirabeau Lamar.

B   Amelia Earhart was a pioneer in the field of aviation.

C   Larry DiLoreto is a baseball fanatic.

D   My neighbor is a complete mystery to me.

E   The early failures of John James Audubon gave way to success later in life.

1.   _____. She comes and goes at all hours of the day and night. Believe it or not, I've seen her leaving her apartment in various disguises. She was dressed once as an elderly woman, once as a clown, and another time as a security guard. She has lived across the hall from me for three years, and I don't even know her name.

2.   _____. In his youth, he failed several times as a businessman. He was even jailed in 1819 for failure to pay his debts. Later, his wife worked to support him while he painted highly detailed pictures of the birds he studied. His collection of paintings was published in 1826, earning him fortune and wide acclaim. He is known to this day as America's most famous naturalist and artist.

3.   _____. Every year, he gets season tickets for both major league and minor league games. He attends every game and cheers wildly, as if the outcome depends on how much noise he can make. He keeps scorecards that chart the statistics of each player. If you ask him, he can tell you the likelihood of any certain pitcher striking out any certain batter.

4.   _____. While traveling in 1838, he came upon a beautiful countryside filled with buffalo. When he became president of the Republic of Texas later that year, he formed a planning committee to build the capital in the spot which he'd found so beautiful. Sam Houston, the previous president, was strongly opposed to this idea. He wanted to have the capital in Houston. Lamar began construction without approval from either Houston or from his own planning committee.

5.   _____. As a passenger on a flight in 1928, she became the first woman to cross the Atlantic Ocean by air. In 1932 she became the first woman to fly across the Atlantic Ocean alone and established a new record for the crossing: 13 hours and 30 minutes. In 1935 she became the first woman to fly over the Pacific Ocean, crossing from Hawaii to California. She was well on her way to making her first flight around the world in 1937; however, her plane disappeared on the final leg of her journey.

C Apply

Write a topic sentence for each of the following paragraphs.

1. _____. The two used to run races in the backyard when they were little girls. When Amy and Lisa got a little older, they raced their bicycles up and down the road, resulting in a lot of skinned knees and anger. Both girls did very well in school, competing with each other for the highest grades. Now they're adults and work as salespeople at rival companies.

   _____

2. _____. The neighbors' dog barked on and off for hours. Someone's car alarm kept going off in the street. Gail's bed began to feel lumpy and uncomfortable. Around three o'clock, just as she was finally drifting off to sleep, she was awakened by a crash in the other room. The cat had knocked a plate off the kitchen counter.

   _____

3. _____. For breakfast, he eats frosted cereal on which he sprinkles extra sugar. Of course, Matt takes his coffee with several spoonfuls of sugar, too. He has dessert after every meal. Dessert usually includes a piece of cake or a few cookies. In his pockets he carries hard candies, which he pops into his mouth throughout the day.

   _____

4. _____. The well-loved tale, "Snow White," shows us how destructive vanity can be. "The Frog Prince" teaches us that a person needs to stay true to her word. She also needs to be kind to everyone, because frogs might turn out to be princes. The tale of "Pinocchio," of course, teaches us that we should not tell lies.

   _____

5. _____. Plants add color and life to every room in a house. At night, they release extra oxygen into the air. This oxygen is good for our bodies while we sleep. Some plants even have medicinal properties. If you cut an aloe leaf open and squeeze its gel onto a cut or a burn, it will aid in the healing process.

   _____

D Check Up

Read each paragraph below. Choose its topic sentence.

1. _____. She plans to turn her dining room into a nursery and make a dining area in her kitchen. She wants to paint a mural on one of the nursery walls. She also intends to put a soft carpet on the floor and make curtains for the windows. If she has time, she wants to rearrange and paint her own bedroom, too.

   A Nina's apartment building was built in 1910.

   B Nina has a lot of redecorating to do before her baby is born.

   C Nina's apartment used to be part of a nursery school.

   D Nina is an excellent painter and craftsperson.

2. _____. You are not allowed to pick up the common pile of cards until you have a certain number of points in your hand. Jokers and twos are wild. Red threes must be set to the side. Your canasta, a set of seven cards of the same face value, can either be "dirty" or "clean." If you don't remember all of these rules, you might wind up scoring negative points!

   F Canasta is more difficult than bridge or poker.

   G If you are not the one to shuffle the deck of cards, you should always ask to "cut the deck."

   H The Canasta championships are being held in Miami this year.

   J Canasta is a difficult game for beginners because there are so many rules to remember.

3. _____. He is going to sleep late and wake up without an alarm clock. He's not going to pick up the newspaper but instead will read his book while he has coffee. Then he is going to meet two of his friends in the park; they'll kick a soccer ball around for a while. He'll have a nice dinner out with these friends, and then they'll catch a movie.

   A Francis used to play soccer professionally.

   B Francis lives in the same town where he grew up.

   C Francis has been laid off from his job of 22 years.

   D Francis has a relaxing day planned for Saturday.

Finding the Topic Sentence

Many writers use a topic sentence to communicate the main idea of a paragraph. When placed at the beginning of the paragraph, as it is in the example below, a topic sentence leads readers into the content of the paragraph. It gives readers a clear sense of what they are about to read.

> <u>The day spa downtown offers a variety of ways for you to pamper yourself.</u> For example, it offers several types of body massage, including Swedish massage and Shiatsu. You can try aromatherapy to soothe your nerves or a salt scrub to stimulate your nervous system. If you want to concentrate on pampering particular parts of your body, you can get a facial, a manicure, or a pedicure. If the spa weren't so expensive, I'd be there every day!

After reading the topic sentence, readers expect that the paragraph will give details about the services offered at the spa.

Sometimes, a topic sentence is placed in the middle or at the end of a paragraph. The reader has already read the details of the paragraph, and the topic sentence summarizes or reinforces these details.

> The sun has been setting a little earlier each day. The air is a bit chilly in the mornings and at night. People are starting to bring out their sweaters and light jackets. Some of the leaves have begun to turn yellow and red. Yesterday, I saw apple cider for sale by the side of the road. <u>It seems that autumn has arrived.</u>

Underline the topic sentence in each of the following paragraphs.

1. Frida Kahlo and Diego Rivera were both painters. Kahlo is best known for her colorful self-portraits. Rivera is famous for painting large murals that celebrate Mexico's history and its working class. Kahlo and Rivera were both politically active and were committed to Marxism. They experienced a great deal of turmoil in their personal lives, including a devastating streetcar accident that seriously injured Kahlo and their well-publicized marital problems. Surely, Frida Kahlo and Diego Rivera are one of the most interesting couples in Mexican history.

2. Falling in love and catching the flu have a lot in common. Both love and the flu usually arrive unexpectedly, taking over your life for a while. Your stomach rejects food, making it difficult or impossible to eat. It becomes hard to concentrate on work, or even on a book or a movie. You toss and turn in bed all night; when you do manage to sleep, you have strange, feverish dreams.

B Practice

Read each paragraph below. Choose its topic sentence.

1.   All her life, Susana has been keeping other people's secrets. When she was young, she dutifully hid her older sisters' mischief from her parents. At school, friends always confessed their secret crushes to her, knowing their secrets would be safe. For many years in Hollywood, Susana worked as a personal assistant to movie stars. She had to sign contracts promising not to give out information about the movie stars to anyone. Now she works for the government, but she won't tell us exactly what she does.

    A For many years in Hollywood, Susana worked as a personal assistant to movie stars.

    B Now she works for the government, but she won't tell us exactly what she does.

    C At school, friends always confessed their secret crushes to her, knowing their secrets would be safe.

    D All her life, Susana has been keeping other people's secrets.

2.   The ancient Mayan people built awe-inspiring pyramids from stones that must have been hauled hundreds or thousands of miles. Today, we have no idea how they managed to do that. The calendar developed by the Mayans was more precise than the one we use today. It is thought by some that the Mayan drawings widely believed to picture human sacrifice are actually depicting the world's first heart surgeries. While we can't make dental fillings that last more than twenty years or so, a Mayan skull has been found with fillings still in its teeth after thousands of years. The Mayans were so advanced that we still haven't caught up with all of their technology.

    F The ancient Mayan people built awe-inspiring pyramids from stones that must have been hauled hundreds or thousands of miles.

    G The calendar developed by the Mayans was more precise than the one we use today.

    H The Mayans were so advanced that we still haven't caught up with all of their technology.

    J It is thought by some that the Mayan drawings widely believed to picture human sacrifice are actually depicting the world's first heart surgeries.

Apply

Write a topic sentence for each of the following paragraphs.

1. _____. You should wear eye protection to prevent a sliver of wood from flying into your eye. Safety goggles or a clear plastic face shield will work as protection. You should also wear a dust mask to avoid inhaling too much sawdust. Always be aware of where your hands are in relation to the moving blade. When using a table saw or a band saw, use a pushstick to guide the wood, rather than letting your hands get too close to the blade.

   _____

   _____

2. The reservoir was running low. The streets all looked dry and dusty, and the grass in the park was withered. Residents were no longer allowed to water their lawns. People were stocking their kitchens with gallons of bottled water. The mayor asked that people do whatever they could to conserve water. _____.

   _____

   _____

3. _____. If Karen loves a certain book or painting, chances are that Jonas hates it. At the movies, Karen loves romantic films while Jonas won't watch anything without lots of guns and car chases. They have opposing political views, and they never vote for the same candidate in an election. They can't even agree on how in the world they got to be friends.

   _____

   _____

4. There was no one at the front desk when we arrived, and we had to wait in the lobby for fifteen minutes. Then we discovered that they had gotten our reservation wrong. When we were finally shown to our room, we were horrified to see a cockroach scurrying across the floor. Our windows opened onto a noisy and trash-filled alley. The shower was just a cold trickle of water, and the drain was clogged with hair. _____.

   _____

   _____

D Check Up

Read each paragraph below. Choose its topic sentence.

1. Many families throw away plastic, glass, and paper products that could easily be recycled. As a nation, we generate a huge amount of trash and don't know what to do with it. Our landfills are becoming too large to handle. Much of our soil is becoming polluted. _____.

    A Individually and collectively, we need to put more effort into recycling.

    B Our country needs to build larger landfills.

    C The trash collection industry is growing in leaps and bounds.

    D When given the choice, you should always opt for a plastic grocery bag.

2. Mamma Mia's has just added an "open microphone" Monday night to their popular weekly music schedule. _____. Customers have already become hooked on Folk Music Tuesday and Jazz Wednesday. Thursday is salsa night, complete with dance instruction for those who arrive early enough. Weekends are filled with fun, too. On Fridays, local rock bands are spotlighted, and Saturday nights are reserved for the performances of major national acts.

    F You can improve your dancing at Mamma Mia's.

    G Mamma Mia's is closed on Sundays.

    H Now Mamma Mia's offers something different every night of the week.

    J Mamma Mia's is named for a song by the Swedish pop group Abba.

3. College students from all over the world come and spend six months as volunteers for the Children's Aid program. They claim that they'll never forget the wonderful experience of building schools and teaching in them. The local residents have really enjoyed getting to know the volunteers, whom they treat as guests. The children are thrilled by all of the attention, and their parents are thrilled about the great education. _____.

    A College programs can offer unique ways for young people to travel.

    B It takes a lot of money to build a school.

    C The Children's Aid program is getting great reviews from everyone involved.

    D The Children's Aid program was founded in 1986.

Supporting Sentences

While a topic sentence states a general main idea, **supporting sentences** provide details to complete the picture. Writers use different types of supporting sentences, depending on what kind of idea they wish to communicate.

Often, a writer wishes to persuade the reader to agree with his or her opinions. In this case, the supporting sentences might be **reasons** why the writer feels as he or she does about an issue.

> Vote "no" on Proposition 22, which would allow fast food and retail chains to open in our neighborhood. After one or two chain stores open, they will spread like wildfire. They will rob our neighborhood of its unique flavor. Soon our streets will look just the same as any streets in any town in the country. Worst of all, the small mom-and-pop drug stores and hamburger stands will be forced out of business by the large, corporate-run competitors.

Sometimes, a writer simply wishes to communicate factual information. In this case, the supporting sentences might contain **facts and figures.**

> To lose weight, burn more calories than you consume each day. If you jog for half an hour and then eat a slice of cheese pizza, the ratio of calorie consumption to calorie burning is equal. A slice of cheese pizza is approximately 250 calories, which is the amount burned by jogging. If you jog for ten extra minutes, you will burn 82.5 more calories and therefore be on the plus side. Other good forms of exercise are bicycling, which burns 563 calories per hour, and jumping rope, which burns 704 calories per hour.

Decide whether the supporting sentences in the following paragraph supply facts and figures or reasons. Write *Facts and Figures* or *Reasons* on the line.

1. You should not participate in the annual running of the bulls in Pamplona, Spain. You would be in danger of being gored by a bull's horn, which has happened to plenty of participants over the years. You would also be subject to injury from the wild crowds of people who fill the streets and sidewalks. Furthermore, bull running is somewhat cruel to the bulls, and attending the event would count as support for the mistreatment of animals.

   _____

B Practice

The purpose of some paragraphs is to create a vivid picture of a place and/or an event. A paragraph with this purpose is usually developed using **sensory details.**

> Our town's Fourth of July festival was a delight for the senses. An enormous crowd filled the town square as the sun went down. Smells of fried dough and grilled sausages wafted through the air. Pealing bells and calls of street vendors echoed off the ancient stone buildings. When the evening grew darker, an enormous boom rang out, and the first of the brilliant fireworks lit up the sky.

Other paragraphs support the main idea with **examples.**

> Many of New York City's visitors never venture off the island of Manhattan; they are missing out on the great sights of the four other boroughs. You can't see a Yankee game in Manhattan; you need to ride up to the Bronx, where you can also visit the Bronx Zoo. The borough of Queens is an important place for art, being the permanent home of the P.S.1 Contemporary Art Center and the temporary home of the world-famous Museum of Modern Art. From the Brooklyn Bridge to Coney Island, Brooklyn has a whole world to offer the visitor. And many New Yorkers will tell you that no visit to their city is complete without a ferry ride to Staten Island.

Read the paragraph below. Decide how it is developed, and circle either *examples* or *sensory details*. Then read the sentences below and choose the one that best develops the paragraph.

1.   The bakery was about to open for the day. _____. There was a delicious aroma of freshly baked bread. In the glass-front cases sat rows of muffins, buttery croissants, and colorful fruit tarts. As soon as the baker unlocked the doors, a stream of early morning customers poured in, filling the shop with pleasant chatter.

This paragraph is developed using (examples, sensory details).

A Therese would be late for work if she waited much longer.

B The owner of the bakery had moved here from Hungary five years earlier.

C The air inside was warm and steamy from the ovens.

C ▶ Apply

Following the directions in parentheses, write one more supporting sentence for each of the following paragraphs.

1.   I think that Grandma should go ahead and marry that nice man she met on the cruise. He's very intelligent, and they have great conversations about politics and culture. He loves to travel, and she's been looking for someone to see the world with. They could live in his house, which is only 45 minutes from ours. _____. (Add a reason.)

_____

_____

2.   The adult education classes at the community college draw quite a diverse group of students. Nearly 20 percent of them were born outside the United States. Racially, they are mixed, with 40 percent white, 30 percent African American, 15 percent Hispanic, 8 percent Asian American, and the rest Native American. About half of the students are in their late teens and early twenties. Ages of the other students vary between 26 and 68. _____. (Add a sentence with an imaginary fact or figure.)

_____

_____

3.   There are many ways to work exercise into a busy day. In a tall building, you can opt for the stairs instead of the elevators. If you have a few extra minutes before an appointment, you can descend the stairs and climb them again. You can always get off the bus or subway one stop early and walk the rest of the way. _____. (Add a sentence with an example.)

_____

_____

4.   We were in the front row at the rock concert, right in front of the stage. The music was loud and explosive, throbbing inside our heads. The crowd was roaring. We could smell perfume, cigarette smoke, and sweat in the air all around us. Some sweat even flew toward us in large droplets from the bobbing head of the guitarist onstage. _____. (Add a sentence with a sensory detail.)

_____

_____

D Check Up

Read each topic sentence. Then choose the answer that best develops the topic sentence.

1. My friend Richard is truly a jack-of-all-trades.

   A His father was a policeman, as was his grandfather. Police work runs in his family.

   B When I met him, he was working in a bank and crafting silver jewelry in his spare time. Now he's working as a locksmith and helping with his wife's catering business.

   C I don't know what career to choose for myself. I seem to have a little skill in many areas. My sister, Ruth, is the same way.

   D Richard got married when he was just eighteen years old. All of his friends tried to talk him out of it, saying that he was too young.

2. We made camp in a forest by a trickling stream.

   F Someday, we'd like to build a log cabin in the forest. A simple life away from the city would be so satisfying.

   G My husband brags that he can set up a tent in under three minutes. But more than once, his tents have collapsed on top of us during the night.

   H It's hard to get a good night's sleep when you're camping. There are biting mosquitoes and strange noises in the forest.

   J The night was clear and cool; stars shone brightly overhead. Our campfire crackled and sparked, smelling pleasantly of wood smoke.

3. Many grand schemes have been suggested to solve the pollution crisis in Mexico City.

   A It is impossible to get a tally of the exact population of Mexico City. The population is estimated at 20–25 million people.

   B Pollution is a problem that affects all of us. The quality of our lives, and of our children's lives, depends on how we handle the issue of pollution.

   C One plan involved using fleets of helicopters to sweep the smog away. Another suggestion involved exploding a hole in the ring of mountains that surround the city.

   D Mexico City is the capital of Mexico. Many Mexicans refer to the city as the Distrito Federal (Federal District) or D.F. for short.

A Introduce

Recognizing Sequence

The purpose of some paragraphs is to describe events in a story. The story might be true or it might be fictional, but it always includes events that happen in a certain order. The order of events is the **sequence** of the narration.

Some paragraphs are concerned with describing steps in a process. These paragraphs, like those that tell a story, must be presented in an order that shows which event happened first, next, and so on.

> If you get a splinter in your finger, try to remove it as soon as possible. Before you begin your mini-surgery, sterilize a pair of tweezers by wiping the ends with rubbing alcohol. Then wash your hands with soap and water, giving special attention to the area around the splinter. Next, grab the splinter with the ends of the sterile tweezers, and pull it out in the same direction as it went in. Gently squeeze the area where the splinter was, in order to encourage slight bleeding which releases any leftover particles of the splinter. Finally, wash the area again and cover it with a bandage.

Read the paragraph and answer each of the questions.

> The movie plot was conventional, but I got caught up in it anyway. It began by introducing a young boy, Freddie, who loved to play soccer, and his pretty, single mom. Next, we saw the new soccer coach, a handsome man with a heart of gold, arrive in town. Under the new coach, the soccer team started winning all their matches. After they won the game that put them in the championships, the coach and the mom professed their love for each other. But then the coach suddenly had to leave town, leaving both Freddie and his mom heartbroken. The soccer team went to the championships and played badly; they were down by four goals at halftime. Then, out of the blue, the coach showed up and revived everyone's spirits. Finally, Freddie scored the goal that won the game, and the coach and the mom kissed each other.

1. What happened just before the coach and the mom professed their love for each other?

   _____

2. What happened after the team was down by four goals at the championships?

   _____

B ▶ Practice

Sometimes, when writing a paragraph in sequence, a writer will include key words to make the order of events clear. Words such as *first, initially, second, next, then, after that, last,* and *finally* help to indicate the time order in a narrative or process.

> When the last customer leaves the café at night, Monica begins her closing chores. <u>First</u>, she wipes down all of the tables and countertops. <u>Second</u>, she puts all of the chairs up on the tables and sweeps the floor. <u>Next</u>, she takes the garbage and the items for recycling out to the alley. <u>Then</u> she empties out the cash register, counts the money, and puts it into the safe. <u>After that</u>, she checks to make sure that all of the appliances are shut off. <u>Finally</u>, she turns out the lights, leaves, and locks the door behind her.

Read the topic sentence of each paragraph and the four sentences below it. Fill in the blank spaces with the letters of the correct sentences to create a paragraph with a sequence that makes sense.

1. The midday meal was always an orderly affair at my grandmother's house

    in Venezuela. Initially, _____. Next, _____. Then, _____. Last, _____.

    A my aunts would clear away the soup bowls and bring out the meat and rice, which we would devour in silence.

    B we would finish up with small dishes of ice cream or sugared fruit.

    C we would all take our places, and my grandmother would say grace.

    D we would eat our soup, which was usually vegetable-based and always delicious.

2. The babysitter showed Gavin how to do her famous floating egg trick.

    First, _____. Next, _____. After that, _____. Finally, _____.

    F she rinsed out a large mayonnaise jar and removed the label.

    G she gently dropped the egg into the salt water and pointed out to Gavin how it floated to the surface.

    H she filled the jar halfway with hot water and stirred in eight tablespoons of salt.

    J she poured regular tap water over the egg; the egg remained floating in the middle of the jar!

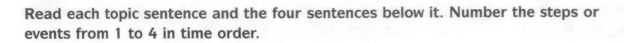

C Apply

Read each topic sentence and the four sentences below it. Number the steps or events from 1 to 4 in time order.

1. Getting your blood drawn is no fun, but at least it doesn't take very long.

    _____ She finds the vein on the inside of your elbow, sterilizes the area, and inserts the needle.

    _____ The technician begins by tying a rubber tourniquet around your arm to control the blood flow.

    _____ Withdrawing the needle, she covers the site with a sterile bandage and removes the tourniquet.

    _____ She draws back on the plunger, filling the tube with your blood.

2. After the flight crew had gotten everybody settled, we began our journey.

    _____ When our turn came, the engines powered up and we began to speed down the runway.

    _____ The wheels lifted, and the plane rose up into the air.

    _____ We backed slowly and smoothly away from the passenger loading gate.

    _____ The plane taxied around and took its place behind the other airplanes waiting to take off.

3. If you have only a day to spend in Zacatecas, I would recommend the following sightseeing plan.

    _____ In the morning, while you are fresh, climb up to the old silver mine and take a guided tour.

    _____ Finally, enjoy the big lunch and the siesta that you've earned!

    _____ When you come out of the mine, take a bus ride across the valley, and visit the museums and historical sites on the other side.

    _____ When you've had your fill of history, descend the steep slopes on foot and come back to the center of town.

4. The orchestra was about to play their big number.

    _____ Eventually, the whole orchestra, including French horns, trombones, and drums, was making a joyful noise.

    _____ Soon after, the reedy voices of oboes and clarinets joined the violins.

    _____ The opening notes were sounded by the violins.

    _____ The conductor rapped gently on the music stand with his baton, calling the musicians to attention.

D Check Up

One sentence is missing from each of the following paragraphs. Choose the sentence that logically completes the sequence.

1.   Wolfgang Amadeus Mozart skyrocketed to classical music fame at a very young age. In fact, at the age of five, he was already playing the violin quite well and composing small musical works. When he was six years old, he was asked to perform for the Empress of Austria. _____. By the time Mozart was fifteen years old, his place in music history had been secured.

   A   Mozart was born in Austria in 1756.

   B   At the tender age of ten, he embarked on a three-year European concert tour.

   C   Mozart truly defines the term "child prodigy."

   D   He died while still a young man, at the age of thirty-five.

2.   The way that we handle tooth problems has changed a lot throughout the ages. Ancient Egyptians believed that a mixture of onions, spices, and incense would cure a toothache. In the Middle Ages, people believed that uttering the name of Apollonia, the patron saint of dentistry, would cure a person of his or her toothache. _____. Today, most of us take our aching teeth to the clean, sterile office of our dentist.

   F   We don't have information about the dental hygiene of the ancient cave dwellers.

   G   Although it is commonly believed that George Washington had false teeth made of wood, they were actually made of ivory and other materials.

   H   In modern times, the sound of the dentist's drill makes many people cringe.

   J   In the sixteenth century, people with tooth problems could get their teeth pulled by the same person who dressed their wounds and cut their hair: the local barber.

3.   Anthony complains about writing research papers, but he always makes it look easy. _____. Next, he heads to the library and takes out five or six books on his topic. He reads through the books at his leisure, just skimming through some and making notes on index cards. Then he organizes his index cards into groups and does some further research on the Internet or in journals. When he feels that he has compiled enough information, he sits at his desk and writes an entire draft in one day.

   A   He wastes a little time surfing the Internet, but he always finds the sites he's looking for.

   B   He spends the last week before the due date revising and polishing his draft.

   C   He writes notes on index cards.

   D   First, he selects his topic immediately after getting the assignment.

Identifying an Unrelated Sentence

The Chandler Company treats its employees well. The salaries are generous, and each employee receives a bonus at holiday time. Everyone who works for the company gets full health benefits. <u>Theresa started working at Chandler's last year.</u> The company even provides an excellent day care center, which is available to the children of all employees.

As you read the paragraph above, you probably noticed that the content of the underlined sentence stood out from the rest. Although it touched on the same topic, the Chandler Company, it was not related to the paragraph's main idea, the ways in which the company treats its employees well.

When you compose a paragraph, make sure each sentence belongs in the paragraph. You may want to begin with a topic sentence that states the main idea. As you write, stay focused on the main idea. Avoid adding sentences that do not support it or describe it more fully. After you write a paragraph, review it carefully to be sure that every sentence relates clearly and obviously to the main idea.

Read the following paragraph. Then answer the questions that follow.

Each of the three early car engines had advantages and disadvantages. The cars whose engines ran on electric batteries were clean, quiet, and easy to start, but slow. Cars that ran on steam engines were clean and fast, but their range was limited to about 150 miles. Trains also used steam engines. Cars equipped with gasoline engines were fast and easy to start, and their range was unlimited, but they broke down regularly and were dirty.

1. What is the main idea of this paragraph?

   _____

2. What is a supporting idea that tells more about the main idea?

   _____

3. Which sentence does not tell more about the main idea?

   _____

B Practice

Read each paragraph. Then follow the directions below.

We should all remember our manners when we talk on the phone. Too often, we treat callers with a rudeness we would never use in face-to-face conversations. First, use a pleasant voice on the phone, not too loud or too soft. Give the caller a chance to state the reason why he or she has called. If the person the caller is trying to reach is unavailable, carefully take a message.

1. Choose the main idea of this paragraph.

   A Modern people are less polite than people in earlier times.

   B We should be courteous when using the phone.

2. One of the sentences below is not related closely enough to be included in the above paragraph. Circle the letter of that sentence.

   A Wait until the caller says good-bye before hanging up the phone.

   B People who call during meals can be annoying.

Ellis Island, near New York City, was a busy place in the early part of the twentieth century. About fifteen million immigrants from all over the world passed through it. At Ellis Island, the would-be immigrants were surrounded by noise and confusion. Families speaking many languages waited in long lines until they could be interviewed.

3. Choose the main idea of this paragraph.

   A During the early part of the twentieth century, the officials at Ellis Island were too busy to do a good job.

   B Ellis Island was a busy place during the early part of the twentieth century.

4. One of the sentences below is not related closely enough to be included in the above paragraph. Circle the letter of that sentence.

   A Many immigrants to the United States were from Eastern Europe.

   B American doctors quickly checked the health of the immigrants, looking for problems such as disease or heart trouble.

Read the following paragraphs. If all the sentences are related to the main idea, write *Correct* on the line. If one sentence is unrelated, cross it out.

1.   The ski resort has facilities to please every winter sports lover. For the downhill skier, there are beginner hills as well as hills that challenge the best skiers. If you like cross country skiing, you can set off on the resort's beautiful network of trails. The resort makes snow on days when natural snow is scarce. You can ice-skate on the frozen lake in front of the main lodge.

   _____

2.   A professional nanny is more than just someone who baby-sits a child. A nanny is expected to be one of the child's first teachers, making playtime into learning time. He or she should be energetic, enthusiastic, and good at keeping the child happy. However, caring for a child is not all fun and games. The nanny must be ready to discipline the child in a fair and responsible way. Nannies must communicate well with adults, too, so that parents feel comfortable with the care their children are receiving. All in all, being a nanny is not an easy job.

   _____

3.   The hurricane that hit Hawaiian island Kauai in 1993 was unusually destructive. Its intense winds blew roofs off many houses and public buildings. Perhaps eighty to ninety percent of the homes in one area of the island of Kauai were totally destroyed. The winds flattened forests and fields of sugar cane. Sugar cane is one of Hawaii's most important crops. Along the beach, huge waves swept cars away, washed out roads, and destroyed boats that had been anchored. All told, the hurricane cost about $1.6 billion in damages.

   _____

4.   George Kaufman, a famous playwright, was always worried about his health. One of his best-known plays, *You Can't Take It with You*, was recently put on by the Westview Little Theater. He was so nervous that he refused to touch doorknobs, which he saw as covered with germs. In his nightmares, he saw himself the victim of all kinds of serious diseases. Kaufman was constantly calling his doctors about real or imagined problems. Because he feared that he was losing his teeth, he saw his dentist about six times every year. Because he thought he was going blind, he bought several pairs of glasses, each one with a different correction.

   _____

D Check Up

Read each paragraph. Then choose the sentence that does not belong.

1.   **1.** Music has the ability to affect our emotions. **2.** Psychologists tell us that fast, high-pitched music creates a happy, energetic feeling in most people. **3.** Conversely, music that is slow and low-pitched makes us feel sad. **4.** The most popular radio station in our city plays music that is labeled "easy listening."

   A Sentence 1

   B Sentence 2

   C Sentence 3

   D Sentence 4

2.   **1.** One of the privileges of holding a top government office is the opportunity to live in a mansion at voter expense. **2.** The U.S. president lives in the magnificent White House in Washington, D.C. **3.** The city of Washington, D.C., was designed by engineer and architect Pierre L'Enfant. **4.** Since the 1970s, a fine Victorian home in Washington has been the residence of the U.S. vice president.

   F Sentence 1

   G Sentence 2

   H Sentence 3

   J Sentence 4

3.   **1.** Many people doodle when they talk on the phone or listen to a lecture. **2.** A simple doodle may offer a glimpse into your personality, or so some people think. **3.** One study linked doodles made of single lines or unattached shapes with people who have a high need for achievement. **4.** The study suggested that people whose doodles feature wavy lines and connected shapes were more likely to be laid back and relaxed.

   A Sentence 1

   B Sentence 2

   C Sentence 3

   D Sentence 4

Transition Words and Phrases

It is the responsibility of the writer to make sure readers understand the relationship between ideas in a paragraph. Merely presenting events, details, or reasons one after the other does not always make connections clear. When you write paragraphs, use transition words to connect one sentence to the next.

Read the following paragraph. The transitional words that connect the sentences have been underlined.

> Janine wanted to celebrate buying a new house. <u>Therefore</u>, she sent out about fifty invitations for a party. She estimated that about half of the people she had invited would come. <u>For that reason</u>, she bought food and drink for only about thirty people. <u>However</u>, about sixty people showed up at her door that afternoon. <u>Consequently</u>, she had to go to the convenience store for more chips and drinks.

This is a list of commonly used transition words and the connections and relationships they make clear:

Time: after, before, when, as soon as, meanwhile, often, at first, immediately, first, next, last, finally

Place: opposite, in front of, beside, over, below, there, inside, within, outside, around

Cause and Effect: for that reason, as a result, consequently, therefore, because, so

Compare or Contrast: on the other hand, in spite of, similarly, besides, however, nevertheless, even so

Example: for example, for instance

Order of Importance: first, primarily, more important

Conclusion: in summary, in conclusion, finally

Underline the transition word or phrase in each item below. Then circle the letter of the relationship the transition clarifies.

1. The proposed tax increase is unnecessary. Therefore, it should be defeated.
   A example   B time   C cause and effect

2. The day was cold; however, the sun was shining brightly.
   F contrast   G place   H cause and effect

B Practice

Each paragraph below is missing one sentence. Read the four lettered sentences at the top of the page. For each paragraph, choose the sentence that makes the best transition. Write the letter of that sentence on the line.

A In spite of those problems, the family was close and happy.

B For example, he created a government program called the Works Progress Administration to build schools, airports, and public buildings.

C Therefore, Americans flocked to light-hearted movies.

D However, the outbreak of World War II caused the federal government to spend lots of money on war materials.

E As a result, many families were too poor to pay for food or shelter.

1. Many unfortunate events took place just before and during the 1930s. First, the stock market crashed in 1929, causing stockholders to lose a great deal of money. Companies went out of business and millions of workers lost their jobs. On top of those problems, a severe drought turned large areas of the United States into a wasteland where little could grow. _____.

2. Franklin Roosevelt became President of the United States in 1932. He believed that the federal government could help Americans get back on their feet. He created several programs that he thought would improve the situation of American workers. _____.

3. My grandfather lived through the Great Depression. His father lost his job, and the family was forced to move in with relatives. Only one person in the household had a full-time job, so money was tight. The family learned how to make a dollar go a long way. They ate simple food and rarely spent money on entertainment or unnecessary luxuries. _____. Grandfather remembers those days as times when everyone pulled together and felt important to one another.

4. Life was often difficult during the Depression, and people needed relief from their problems. _____. Films that starred Shirley Temple, a young actress with an infectious smile and a can-do attitude, became quite popular. Watching little Shirley sing and dance, Americans could forget their troubles and believe that happier days were on the way.

5. By the end of the 1930s the stock market was once again stable, but unemployment was still high. _____. This created many new jobs in factories, and unemployment declined quickly. In fact, unemployment was soon replaced by a shortage of workers.

C Apply

Read each paragraph. Then choose the transition that works best to complete the paragraph.

1.   When Justine climbed aboard the bus that afternoon, she was hot and tired. It had been a rough day at work, filled with minor frustrations. The bus was crowded and the air conditioning wasn't working. Justine had nowhere to sit, so she clung to the back of a seat and hoped she wouldn't fall whenever the bus jerked to a stop. _____, Justine was happy. She was on her way home at last.

   A Similarly   **B** Even so   **C** For example   **D** For that reason

2.   Eating foods from every basic food group will insure that you get the nutrients you need to stay healthy. _____, fruits are good sources of vitamin C. Dairy products supply vitamins, calcium, and protein. Meats, eggs, and nuts supply protein; breads and cereals supply carbohydrates; and vegetables are excellent sources of vitamins, calcium, and iron.

   F Therefore   **G** On the other hand   **H** Nevertheless   **J** For example

3.   The meal at the expensive restaurant was everything Brian and Stacy could have hoped for. First, the hostess greeted them with a smile and led them to an excellent table by the window. The waiter was helpful and friendly as he answered questions about items on the menu. When the appetizers came, they were delicious, and so was the main course that followed. After finishing the main course, the couple ordered a rich dessert to split. _____, the couple went home, a little poorer but definitely satisfied with their experience.

   A Finally   **B** However   **C** Likewise   **D** For instance

4.   Winds of change were blowing around the world during the eighteenth century. The American colonies revolted against oppressive British rule, and a new nation, the United States of America, was born. _____, the people of France decided that they could no longer endure abuse from their king, so they too revolted.

   F Therefore   **G** First   **H** On the other hand   **J** Similarly

5.   Kate was determined to show her boss that she deserved a raise. She came in early every day and stayed late. Kate made sure that no calls went unreturned and no paperwork was forgotten. She helped her fellow employees if they had problems and tried to make her department run as efficiently as possible. _____, Kate was named Employee of the Month and received a nice raise.

   A For example   **B** As a result   **C** Mainly   **D** Sometimes

Read each paragraph. Then choose the sentence that best fills the blank.

1.   Nothing went according to plan on the Prentiss family's first vacation in years. Their plane was delayed, so they missed their connecting flight. Their luggage went to a different city. The hotel lost their reservations, so they had to spend the first night crowded in a tiny room. _____.

   A Consequently, the Prentiss family enjoyed their trip.

   B Similarly, the Prentiss family enjoyed their trip.

   C In spite of all these problems, the Prentiss family enjoyed their trip.

   D As a result, the Prentiss family enjoyed their trip.

2.   Marilyn made a list of reasons why she should take the new job. It would pay better than her present job and would give her needed experience in her field. Although it involved traveling, the job might lead to greater opportunities. _____.

   F In comparison, when she traveled, she could make new contacts that might prove useful.

   G Besides, when she traveled, she could make new contacts that might prove useful.

   H First, when she traveled, she could make new contacts that might prove useful.

   J Therefore, when she traveled, she could make new contacts that might prove useful.

3.   Team owner Bill Veeck was always inventing ways to bring baseball fans into the ballpark. _____. Another prize was 20,000 orchids. In an early morning game intended to bring women to the ballpark, Veeck gave free admission to women wearing hard hats or welding masks. He had ushers at the game wear nightgowns and serve free coffee and doughnuts.

   A For example, one time he gave away 10,000 cupcakes to a lucky fan.

   B In contrast, one time he gave away 10,000 cupcakes to a lucky fan.

   C At the same time, he once gave away 10,000 cupcakes to a lucky fan.

   D However, one time he gave away 10,000 cupcakes to a lucky fan.

Review

Main Idea and Topic Sentence

In every paragraph, sentences work together to support a single idea, called the **main idea**. Often, one sentence, called the **topic sentence,** states the main idea of the paragraph. When it appears at the beginning of the paragraph, a topic sentence leads readers into the content of the paragraph. A topic sentence in the middle or at the end of a paragraph can summarize or reinforce details presented in the paragraph.

Supporting Sentences

Supporting sentences develop the main idea of a paragraph. Writers use different types of supporting sentences, depending on the kind of idea they are trying to communicate. For example, in paragraphs in which writers wish to voice their opinions about issues, the supporting sentences might present reasons. Facts and figures or examples may be used to develop other paragraphs. When writing descriptive paragraphs, writers often use sentences filled with sensory details.

Sequence

Usually, writers present events in a story in the order, or sequence, in which they happen. We say they tell the story in **time order.** Writers also use time order when they describe the steps of a multistep process in the order in which they happened or should happen. Key words such as *first, initially, second, next, then, after that, last,* and *finally* indicate the order of events or steps in a narrative or a process explanation.

Avoiding Unrelated Sentences

Every sentence in a paragraph should help to develop its main idea. The inclusion of a sentence that does not relate to the main idea only confuses the reader. To avoid unrelated sentences, you may want to begin with a topic sentence that states the main idea and then add only sentences that support it or describe it more fully. After writing the first draft, take time to reread the piece and remove any unrelated sentences.

Transition Words and Phrases

Every sentence in a paragraph must relate not only to the main idea but also to the sentences that come before and after it. Clear writers do more than just present a series of facts and details. They also make connections between them. When you write paragraphs, use transition words such as *meanwhile, often, therefore, on the other hand, nevertheless, however, finally,* and *in conclusion* to connect one sentence to the next.

Read each paragraph. Then choose the sentence that best fills in the blank in the paragraph.

1. _____. As is usual in national celebrations, revelers set off noisy firecrackers. Joyous music fills the air. Also, because this day commemorates the famous shout given by Father Miguel Hidalgo in 1810 to start the War of Independence, shouting is part of the celebration. All over the country can be heard the cry, "Viva Mexico!"

   A Firecrackers are part of every national celebration in most countries, including Mexico.

   B Mexican independence came about after political and economic changes.

   C The day when Mexicans celebrate their independence is a loud one, indeed.

   D Mexico is a fascinating country to visit.

2. _____. His parents, both music-hall performers in London, were very poor. Charlie's mother had a nervous breakdown, and his father died when Charlie was five. Charlie and his brother grew up on the streets, with occasional stays in charity homes.

   F Charlie Chaplin was one of the greatest comic geniuses in film history.

   G Charlie Chaplin won several awards for his portrayal of the "Little Tramp."

   H Audiences love Charlie Chaplin's underdog character, the "Little Tramp."

   J Charlie Chaplin had plenty of early misfortune to draw upon for his "Little Tramp" role.

3. The Franklin family's new puppy has been a lot of trouble. Patches refuses to sleep by himself in the utility room. Instead he cries for hours every night until someone gives in and lets him sleep on one of the beds. He is fascinated by smelly garbage and has been known to strew the trash all over the floor when everyone is gone for the day. He insists on straining at the leash instead of walking calmly beside his owners. _____.

   A Likewise, the Franklins are crazy about their cute little troublemaker.

   B Even so, the Franklins are crazy about their cute little troublemaker.

   C Therefore, the Franklins are crazy about their cute little troublemaker.

   D Finally, the Franklins are crazy about their cute little troublemaker.

Read each topic sentence. Then choose the answer that best develops the topic sentence.

4. Psychologists say that people's personalities can be divided into two major categories.

   F Psychologists sometimes administer personality tests. They use the findings from these tests to help people understand themselves better.

   G Introverts have rich inner lives; they don't need many people or much outside excitement to keep themselves happy and interested. Extroverts are at their best when they can feel the excitement and stimulation of being with other people.

   H My brother Johnny has an outgoing personality. His ease around people makes him a natural salesman.

   J Our moods are always changing. However, our personalities remain fairly constant throughout our lives.

5. To the young man from the small town, the downtown street seemed strange and overwhelming.

   A More people live in the city than live in the country. In fact, in the United States, about 75 percent of the population lives in cities.

   B Sam had come to the city to be interviewed for a new job. His hometown was about 450 miles from the city.

   C Sam felt small and alone when he saw the towering gray buildings everywhere. When he heard the angry roar of the buses and felt the heat from their exhaust push against his body, he longed for his quiet, safe home.

   D Years ago, Chicago was the second largest city in the United States, while New York City was the largest. At that time, Chicago became known as the "Second City."

6. For many reasons, we residents of planet Earth must preserve our rain forests.

   F Rain forests help us by controlling the world's climate. In addition, the plants and animals of the rain forest are proving to be sources of life-saving medicines.

   G Rain forests are found near the equator. The Amazon rain forest in Brazil is the largest in the world.

   H Rain forests are being cut down at an alarming rate all around the world. Many people have no idea how important they are.

   J Tropical rain forests get up to 400 inches of rain every year.

Read each paragraph. Then choose the sentence that does <u>not</u> belong in the paragraph.

7. **1.** The nursery school students were engaged in a variety of activities. **2.** Some children were painting on large sheets of paper attached to easels. **3.** Mrs. Keifer has been a nursery school teacher for over twenty years. **4.** A few children were happily constructing a fort with huge cardboard blocks, while others were playing dress-up.

   A Sentence 1

   B Sentence 2

   C Sentence 3

   D Sentence 4

8. **1.** Hiking is a form of exercise that most people can enjoy with little or no training. **2.** The Appalachian Trail is the most developed long-distance hiking trail in the United States. **3.** The trail is well marked and easy to follow. **4.** Along the trail, from Georgia to Maine, there are plenty of well-maintained shelters where hikers can stop for the night.

   F Sentence 1

   G Sentence 2

   H Sentence 3

   J Sentence 4

9. **1.** The new fall line-up of television shows looks a lot like last year's collection of programs. **2.** For example, one show features an appealing young family with an ever-so-wise mom and a kind-hearted but impractical dad. **3.** Other shows focus on life in a busy city hospital or a gritty city high school. **4.** My favorite show is still *ER* even though it has been on the air for nine years.

   A Sentence 1

   B Sentence 2

   C Sentence 3

   D Sentence 4

Capitalizing Proper Nouns and *I*

Proper nouns name particular persons, places, or things. To set these
names off from other words, they are capitalized. Remember the
following rules of capitalization when you write the names of
particular people or animals.

- **Capitalize names of people.** Capitalize every word and initial in a
  person's name.

  Louisa May Alcott   J. D. Salinger

- **Capitalize titles and abbreviations when they appear before names.** Examples of
  titles are *Doctor* and *Mayor*. Common abbreviations of titles include *Dr., Mr., Mrs.,*
  and *Ms.*

  My new dentist is <u>Dr. Orin</u>.
  Here is a photo of the current coach, <u>Coach Jones</u>.

- **Capitalize words for family relations when they are used with or in place of the
  names of particular people.** If a family title follows a possessive pronoun such as
  my, our, or *your,* it is not capitalized.

  I saw my <u>grandmother</u> at <u>Aunt Theresa's</u> house.
  My <u>father</u> loves to garden, but <u>Mom</u> is not interested.

Remember that the pronoun *I* should always be capitalized.

Circle every word that should be capitalized in each of the following sentences.

1. Did uncle austin make an appointment with dr. klein?

2. My mother and i planned a surprise party for aunt jackie.

3. You should read this article by j.r quinn.

4. This beautiful rose was named in honor of princess diana.

5. The winning ticket was purchased by mr. tony asaro.

6. I will introduce you to the store manager, ms. lynne martin.

7. That writer, sir arthur conan doyle, created the character of sherlock holmes.

8. When cousin amy went on vacation, she bought gifts for the whole family.

B Practice

Read each of the following items. Capitalize words wherever necessary. Write *Correct* on the line if the item is written correctly.

1. my favorite niece _____

2. president richard m. nixon _____

3. Julia d. Grant _____

4. aunt Peggy _____

5. dr. william stewart _____

6. justice Ruth bader ginsberg _____

7. our local doctor _____

8. johann sebastian bach _____

9. james a. brennan _____

10. cousin luke _____

11. ms. erica kane _____

Read each of the following sets of sentences. Choose the sentence with correct capitalization.

12. **A** One of my favorite authors is diana wynne jones.

    B One of my favorite authors is Diana Wynne Jones.

    C One of My favorite Authors is Diana Wynne Jones.

13. **F** Write a Letter to your Senator.

    G Write a letter to your Senator.

    H Write a letter to your senator.

14. **A** Our whole Family had a good time at grandpa's 80th birthday.

    B Our whole family had a good time at Grandpa's 80th birthday.

    C Our whole family had a good time at Grandpa's 80th Birthday.

C Apply

Each sentence below has capitalization errors. Rewrite each sentence correctly.

1. We rented the Apartment from mr. kevin hayes.

   _____

2. Will kwame and isaac be working on the project with us?

   _____

3. This is an excellent Biography of general john j. pershing.

   _____

4. Does cindy wiles ever arrive on time?

   _____

5. My Sister and i were always getting into trouble with our Neighbor, mr. rufus.

   _____

6. Tell private cox to report to sergeant riley.

   _____

For each item, choose the name with correct capitalization.

7. **A** uncle Louis
   B Dr. Edward Teller
   C Sasha wyler
   D mayor Flynn

8. **F** grandma Vivian
   G professor Lian
   H Ms. Nicole Milet
   J major William Parker

9. **A** t. s. Eliot
   B Congressman Tyler
   C your Cousin
   D Senator b. Boxer

10. **F** Mr. Ruben o. Sanchez
    G Kristi ann reyes
    H Officer blake
    J Mayor Chen Liu

Read each set of sentences below. Choose the sentence that has correct capitalization.

1. **A** Our next City Councilwoman will be Anna Henderson!

   B Ask the Policeman for directions to the concert hall.

   C We had lunch with Aunt Rachel at an elegant restaurant.

   D My Father and uncle Dave go camping every summer.

2. **F** My great-grandpa, josiah Smith, was the first settler in the area.

   G I was told that aunt Rita saw Elvis presley in concert twice!

   H Please stand when the Judge enters the court.

   J My mother had a long talk with Principal Alves.

3. **A** Dr. Avi Cohn is an excellent Surgeon.

   B Make the check out to Mary Clare Ames.

   C Our Loan Officer is Tanya Wills.

   D The car that uncle Gabe just bought was stolen last night.

4. **F** Your training class will be led by Mr. Chase Krandall.

   G My friends and i have decided to vote for julio t. Cannon.

   H The lead singer for my band was my Cousin.

   J My neighbor, mrs. linda chen, goes jogging every morning.

Read each sentence and look at the underlined words. Choose the answer that is written correctly for the underlined words.

5. I recently read a biography of <u>admiral William f. Halsey</u>.

   A admiral William F. Halsey

   B Admiral William F. Halsey

   C admiral william f. Halsey

   D Correct as it is

6. One of the greatest sports car racers of all time is <u>a. j. Foyt</u>.

   F A. J. Foyt

   G A. J. foyt

   H A. j. Foyt

   J Correct as it is

7. Would you bring <u>Grandma mariel</u> a cup of tea?

   A grandma Mariel

   B Grandma Mariel

   C grandma mariel

   D Correct as it is

8. My friend, <u>Professor ivy depner</u>, will teach this class.

   F professor Ivy Depner

   G Professor ivy Depner

   H Professor Ivy Depner

   J Correct as it is

Capitalizing Proper Nouns and Proper Adjectives

Remember the following rules of capitalization when you write these types of proper nouns and proper adjectives.

- **Capitalize names of days, holidays, and months.** Do not capitalize the names of the seasons.

    Thursday   Thanksgiving   November   winter

- **Capitalize the names of cities, states, countries, and continents.**

    Chicago   Illinois   Poland   Asia

- **Capitalize the names of streets, buildings, institutions, and bridges.**

    Ash Road   Coit Tower   Ohio University   Key Bridge

- **Capitalize geographical names.** Capitalize words such as *north, east,* and *west* only when they refer to a section of the country.

    We camped in the <u>White Mountains</u> in the <u>Northeast</u>.
    The <u>Platte River</u> winds across the <u>southern</u> part of the state.

- **Capitalize the names of languages and peoples and the proper adjectives associated with them.** Proper adjectives are words made from proper nouns. Often, the proper noun is changed slightly and an ending is added to make it into a proper adjective.

    Most <u>Americans</u> speak the <u>English</u> language. (*Americans* comes from the proper noun *America; English* comes from the proper noun *England.*)

Read each of the following items. Capitalize words wherever necessary. Write *Correct* on the line if the item is written properly.

1. groundhog day   _____

2. pittsburgh, pennsylvania   _____

3. clayton building   _____

4. lake huron   _____

5. french bread   _____

6. tower bridge   _____

7. eastern missouri   _____

8. hills and valleys   _____

B ► Practice

- **Capitalize the names of government agencies.**

  Congress   Internal Revenue Service

- **Capitalize the names of clubs, organizations, and businesses.**

  Vale Glee Club   Republican Party   Viceroy Corporation

- **Capitalize the names of historical and special events.**

  Civil War   World Series

- **If a proper noun has more than one word, capitalize all important words,** but do not capitalize short articles and prepositions such as *the, of,* or *in.*

  Fourth of July   War of the Roses

Read each of the following sets of sentences. Choose the sentence that is capitalized correctly.

1. **A** The Royal Gorge bridge crosses the Arkansas river.

   B The Royal Gorge Bridge crosses the Arkansas River.

   C The royal Gorge Bridge crosses the Arkansas river.

2. **F** My neighbor has worked for the federal aviation Administration since June.

   G My neighbor has worked for the Federal Aviation Administration since june.

   H My neighbor has worked for the Federal Aviation Administration since June.

3. **A** First we headed south on Duncan Street; then we turned west toward the river.

   B First we headed South on Duncan Street; then we turned West toward the river.

   C First we headed South on Duncan Street; then we turned west toward the River.

Circle the words that should be capitalized in each sentence.

4. The united states census bureau counts the nation's population every ten years.

5. On tuesday, we received travel information from the newton chamber of commerce.

6. The special olympics will be held at the fulton center this weekend.

7. My uncle worked for the moore trucking company for many years.

8. The zephyr appliance company on sidney street is having a sale on refrigerators.

◆C Apply

Rewrite each of the following sentences using correct capitalization.

1. The bus crossed the mackinac bridge and headed into northern michigan.

   _____

2. My brother graduated from hudson high school last june.

   _____

3. The countries of brazil and argentina are in south america.

   _____

4. Members of the united auto workers marched in the parade on labor day.

   _____

5. Joshua spent two years as a volunteer for the peace corps in nicaragua.

   _____

6. We stayed at the mountain view inn near pikes peak last summer.

   _____

7. My mother raises african violets.

   _____

8. The imperial carpet cleaning company did an excellent job on our oriental rug.

   _____

9. The kentucky derby is run on the first saturday in may.

   _____

10. The climate in the southwest is drier than that of the northwest.

    _____

11. Some pictures on the walls of european caves were painted during the stone age.

    _____

12. The curran theatre is on geary street in the city of san francisco.

    _____

D Check Up

Read each set of sentences. Choose the sentence that has correct capitalization.

1. **A** The blue eyes of my Siamese Cat are beautiful.

   B A late winter blizzard has shut down the Northeast.

   C The Spring classes begin on Monday, march 8.

   D I wonder which teams will play in the Super bowl this year.

2. **F** My brother plays saxophone at the House of Jazz.

   G The tailwinds bicycle Club sponsors a race every summer.

   H We hiked in the great smoky mountains in Eastern Tennessee.

   J I baked some Swedish Meatballs for the party.

3. **A** The university of Notre Dame is famous for its football team.

   B A decision was handed down by the supreme Court today.

   C The Franklin Lumber Company is not open on Sunday.

   D The Continent of Australia is also a Country.

4. **F** The cliff dwellings in mesa verde national park are fascinating.

   G The Leaning Tower Of Pisa is in Italy.

   H She was elected to the house of Representatives.

   J The Texas State Fair is the largest in the United States.

Read each sentence and look at the underlined words. Choose the answer that is written correctly for the underlined words.

5. The <u>Month of June</u> is a popular time for weddings.

   A month of june

   B month of June

   C Month of june

   D Correct as it is

6. Citizens are encouraged to fly their flags on <u>flag day</u>.

   F Flag day

   G flag Day

   H Flag Day

   J Correct as it is

7. The company has moved to <u>Denver, Colorado</u>.

   A Denver, colorado

   B denver, Colorado

   C denver, colorado

   D Correct as it is

8. The <u>Columbia river</u> is broad and deep.

   F Columbia River

   G columbia River

   H columbia river

   J Correct as it is

Capitalizing First Words, Titles, and Abbreviations

Every sentence must begin with a capital letter.

 That is a stunning sweater.   When did you buy it?

The first word of every quotation should be capitalized.

 "Where is the nearest gas station?" asked Pauline.
 Orval replied, "Turn left at the next intersection."

The first word, the last word, and any other important words in a title must be capitalized. Words like *the, in, for, from, a, an, of, on,* or *by* are not capitalized unless they appear first or last in the title.

 The Mystery of the Blue Train (book)
 Sports Illustrated (magazine)
 "Smoke and Steel" (poem)

Many abbreviations should be capitalized. Abbreviations are shortened forms of words or phrases.

 Send the entry form to P.O. Box 73902.
 Devon works the 11:00 P.M. to 7:00 A.M. shift.

Read each pair of sentences. Then circle the letter of the sentence with correct capitalization.

1. **A** The flight arrived in Honolulu at 4:15 p.m.

   B The flight arrived in Honolulu at 4:15 P.M.

2. **A** This magazine, *Garden Gate*, contains useful gardening tips.

   B This magazine, *garden gate,* contains useful gardening tips.

3. **A** "Did you get the newspaper today?" asked my neighbor.

   B "did you get the newspaper today?" asked my neighbor.

4. **A** twigs and small branches covered the ground after the windstorm.

   B Twigs and small branches covered the ground after the windstorm.

5. **A** One firefighter shouted, "Stand back from the burning building!"

   B one firefighter shouted, "stand back from the burning building!"

6. **A** Our business cards had p.o. box 1330 printed in red letters.

   B Our business cards had P.O. Box 1330 printed in red letters.

B Practice

Correct the capitalization errors in the following titles. If a title is capitalized properly, write *Correct* on the line.

1. "With or without you" (song) _____

2. *the fellowship of the ring* (book and movie) _____

3. "Not in vain" (poem) _____

4. *The News Herald* (newspaper) _____

5. *Home improvement* (television program) _____

6. "Hearts and hands" (short story) _____

7. *Taste of Home* (magazine) _____

8. *A chorus line* (play) _____

9. *shadows on the rock* (book) _____

Look at the numbered, underlined parts in the following paragraph. Choose the correct answer for each underlined part.

(10)　　　Some people enjoy movies. <u>whether it is 7:00 p.m. or 2:00 a.m.</u>, their eyes are
(11) glued to the screen. They remember every detail of <u>*raiders of the lost ark*</u> or
(12) <u>*an officer and a gentleman*</u>. If you ask these fans about their favorite movie, they
(13) might <u>answer, "We love all movies!"</u>

10. A Whether it is 7:00 p.m. or 2:00 a.m.

    B Whether it is 7:00 P.M. or 2:00 A.M.

    C whether it is 7:00 P.M. or 2:00 A.M.

    D Correct as it is

11. F *Raiders of the lost ark*

    G *Raiders Of The Lost Ark*

    H *Raiders of the Lost Ark*

    D Correct as it is

12. A *An Officer and a Gentleman*

    B *an Officer and a Gentleman*

    C *An Officer and A Gentleman*

    D Correct as it is

13. F answer, "we love all movies!"

    G answer, "We Love All Movies!"

    H answer, "We love all Movies!"

    J Correct as it is

C ◆ Apply

Rewrite each sentence using correct capitalization.

1. "my mailing address is p.o. box 152," said Mrs. Magee.

   _____

2. *the west wing* is Julia's favorite television program.

   _____

3. our neighbors bought tickets to see the stage production of *the lion king.*

   _____

4. she asked, "where is this month's issue of *national geographic*?"

   _____

5. "the show will begin promptly at 8:30 p.m.," said the announcer.

   _____

6. my daughter memorized the poem, "paul revere's ride."

   _____

7. "*to kill a mockingbird* is a powerful book," replied the librarian.

   _____

8. the toddler whined, "grandma, I want more cookies."

   _____

9. at the end of the program, the choir sang Beethoven's "ode to joy."

   _____

10. we always read our local newspaper, *the sun journal.*

    _____

11. "the pit and the pendulum" is one of Poe's scariest short stories.

    _____

12. send the subscription for *archeology today* to p.o. box 515.

    _____

Check Up

Read each set of sentences below. Choose the sentence with correct capitalization.

1. **A** "my subscription to *Better Homes and Gardens* has expired," said Betty.

   B "Think about the cost before you decide," suggested the mechanic.

   C "do you have any ointment?" Ali asked the pharmacist.

   D The nurse said, "this won't hurt a bit."

2. **F** We must leave no later than 6:45 A.M.

   G mortgage payments are sent to p.o. box 56 rather than to a local address.

   H When the alarm rang at 5:15 a.m., I jumped out of bed.

   J "does the early news show start at 7:00 A.M.?" inquired Brian.

3. **A** the movie *jurassic park* has exciting special effects.

   B "There was an interesting article about pollution in the *los angeles times*," commented Eldred.

   C "Is *wheel of fortune* your favorite game show?" asked Mike.

   D Estelle's grandson loves to watch *Sesame Street*.

4. **F** "read the directions first," ordered the manager.

   G The waiter asked, "would you like to see the dessert menu?"

   H "Is the report finished?" the boss asked.

   J *U.S. news and world report* is a weekly news magazine.

5. **A** "show me your passport," demanded the customs official.

   B Henry shouted, "there they are!"

   C The poem, "Mother to Son," expresses hope and courage.

   D A reporter for the *Akron beacon journal* interviewed me today.

6. **F** the coach shouted, "hold onto the football!"

   G The local drama club is presenting *The Sound of Music* this weekend.

   H "Josh likes action movies like *mission impossible*," explained Belinda.

   J Stephanie sang "the yellow Submarine" over and over.

Proper Nouns, Proper Adjectives, and *I*

Capitalize the names of people. Capitalize titles and their abbreviations.

> J. K. Rowling   Queen Elizabeth   Dr. Montoya

Capitalize words for family relations when they are used with or in place of the names of specific people.

> Aunt Julia   Grandpa John   Dad

Capitalize the names of days, months, and holidays.

> Sunday   May   Presidents' Day

Capitalize the names of cities, states, countries, and continents.

> Houston   Minnesota   India   Asia

Capitalize the names of streets, buildings, institutions, and bridges.

> Oak Street   Crystal Palace   Bates College

Capitalize geographical names. Capitalize words such as *north, south,* and *west* only when they refer to a section of the country.

> Lake Michigan   Rocky Mountains   the Southwest

Capitalize the names of languages and peoples and the proper adjectives associated with them.

> Spanish   Canadians   Swiss cheese

Capitalize the names of clubs, organizations, government agencies, and businesses.

> Aces Bridge Club   Central Intelligence Agency

Capitalize the names of historical and special events.

> Revolutionary War   New York World's Fair

Always capitalize the pronoun *I.*

First Words, Titles, and Abbreviations

Begin every sentence with a capital letter.

> Did you buy movie tickets?   They are too expensive.

Capitalize the first word of every direct quotation.

> "The party is tonight, " said Al.   Ben asked, "Are you going?"

Capitalize the first, last, and any other important words in a title.

> *My Fair Lady* (movie)   *Atlantic Monthly* (newspaper)

Capitalize many abbreviations, such as P.O., A.M., and P.M.

Read the following paragraphs and look at their numbered, underlined parts. Choose the answer that is written correctly for each underlined part.

　　　　One day, a hopeful young actor performed a screen test at a movie studio in

(1) the city of <u>hollywood, California</u>. One executive was not impressed with the

(2) young man's performance. After the tryout, he <u>commented, "can't</u> act, slightly bald, dances a little." In later years, this executive may have wanted to take back

(3) his lukewarm review. The young actor, <u>Fred Astaire</u>, became one of the biggest stars of musical comedies in Hollywood.

1. **A** hollywood, california

　　B Hollywood, california

　　C Hollywood, California

　　D Correct as it is

3. **A** Fred astaire

　　B fred Astaire

　　C fred astaire

　　D Correct as it is

2. **F** commented, "Can't

　　G Commented, "Can't

　　H Commented, "can't

　　J Correct as it is

(4) 　　　　In 1896, gold was discovered near the banks of the <u>Yukon river</u>.

(5) When news of the discovery got out, people from<u> all over the World</u>

(6) started rushing <u>North to alaska</u>, hoping to strike it rich in the gold fields. By 1898, thousands of gold seekers were headed home, most of them disappointed and broke.

4. **F** yukon river

　　G yukon River

　　H Yukon River

　　J Correct as it is

6. **F** north to Alaska

　　G North to Alaska

　　H north to alaska

　　J Correct as it is

5. **A** All Over the World

　　B all over the world

　　C All over the World

　　D Correct as it is

(7)   Every March 3, <u>japanese Families</u> observe an unusual holiday called the

(8) <u>doll festival</u>. On that day, families display a special set of dolls, ones that were

(9) given to a girl by her <u>Parents or Grandparents</u> either at birth or on her first birthday. These dolls are elegant works of art, not toys.

7. **A** Japanese Families

     B Japanese families

     C japanese families

     D Correct as it is

9. **A** Parents or grandparents

     B parents or grandparents

     C parents or Grandparents

     D Correct as it is

8. **F** Doll festival

     G doll Festival

     H Doll Festival

     J Correct as it is

(10)   The <u>Brighton Film Society</u> will hold its annual film festival next weekend.

(11) <u>On friday</u> the focus will be on films from Australia. Saturday's films are all from Asia, and the festival ends on Sunday with short subjects produced in Europe.

(12) The award-winning animated film *<u>the meaning of Life</u>* will be shown on Sunday.

10. **F** Brighton Film society

      G Brighton film society

      H brighton film society

      J Correct as it is

12. **F** *The Meaning Of Life*

      G *The Meaning of Life*

      H *The meaning of Life*

      J Correct as it is

11. **A** on Friday

      B on friday

      C On Friday

      D Correct as it is

Choose the sentence that has correct capitalization.

13. A   The Police Officer asked, "what seems to be the problem here?"

    B   The bakery opens at 6:00 A.M.

    C   Keep your muddy shoes off the oriental rug!

    D   Baseball teams start training in the Spring.

14. F   My Sister and I talk on the phone for hours.

    G   Rain is expected today in the midwest.

    H   Keep practicing and you may one day perform at Carnegie hall.

    J   Construction work is causing traffic delays on Elm Street.

15. A   This article describes flowers that grow in North America.

    B   My Brother hopes to be a Professional Golfer some day.

    C   Expect the best from top hat Limousine Service!

    D   I read your ad in the *Montgomery sentinel.*

16. F   Do you know who won the first World series?

    G   my friend is looking for a Summer job.

    H   Drive North over the Aurora Bridge.

    J   The salesclerk said, "This sweater is also available in blue."

17. A   The order was issued by captain Lister.

    B   One of my favorite movies is *casablanca.*

    C   Send the form to P.O. Box 9204.

    D   The State of Wisconsin is famous for its cheese products.

18. F   My Doctor prescribed some medicine for my headaches.

    G   You have to be in excellent physical condition to swim across the English Channel.

    H   My children have fun coloring eggs at easter.

    J   This castle was built in the middle ages.

19. A   The local Police called the Federal bureau of investigation.

    B   Rev. Willis will retire in June.

    C   Let's go out to a Restaurant tonight.

    D   I found the wallet on Sterling avenue.

20. F   I just received my first issue of *Today's Fitness News.*

    G   Do you know aunt Joy's address?

    H   Our flight leaves at 5:35 P.m.

    J   Many Italian Immigrants settled in this part of the City.

End Marks

Period

A period is used at the end of a statement.

> The concert is about to begin.

A period is used at the end of most commands.

> Hand each patron a program before the concert.

Question Mark

A question mark is used at the end of a question.

> What composers will be featured at the concert?

Exclamation Point

An exclamation point is used at the end of an exclamation, that is, a sentence that expresses strong feeling, such as excitement or surprise.

> How beautiful this symphony is!

An exclamation point is also used at the end of a command that expresses a strong or urgent feeling.

> Stop that thief!

Write the correct end mark for each sentence.

1. How often does the oil need to be changed in this car

2. What an incredible performance that was

3. Turn left at the next intersection

4. Get out of my way

5. Do we need to order more paper

6. These library books are due next Thursday

7. My wallet has been stolen

8. Please see me before you go home

9. Run for cover

10. There are three job openings in this department

B ▶ Practice

Decide which end mark, if any, is needed for each sentence.

1. Sign this list if you would like to attend the conference
   A .   B ?   C !   D None

2. The speed limit on this road is thirty miles per hour
   F .   G ?   H !   J None

3. The umpire shouted, "You're out"
   A .   B ?   C !   D None

4. Have you ever served on a jury before
   F .   G ?   H !   J None

5. Wait for me!
   A .   B ?   C !   D None

6. What toppings would you like on your pizza
   F .   G ?   H !   J None

Read each pair of sentences. Circle the letter of the sentence with the correct end mark.

7. **A** You can arrange to have your checks deposited automatically.

   B You can arrange to have your checks deposited automatically?

8. **A** I can't believe what I'm hearing?

   B I can't believe what I'm hearing!

9. **A** Remember to renew your driver's license.

   B Remember to renew your driver's license?

10. **A** When do I get my first paycheck?

    B When do I get my first paycheck!

11. **A** Be home by midnight?

    B Be home by midnight!

12. **A** I locked my keys in the car?

    B I locked my keys in the car!

C ▸ Apply

Different situations are described below. In one sentence, write what you might say in each situation. Use the correct end mark for each sentence.

1. You need catsup for your French fries.

   _____

2. You have just received a birthday present.

   _____

3. You need to tell a clerk why you are returning an item you bought.

   _____

4. You need to warn your guests that the soup you are serving is very hot.

   _____

5. A friend has just told you she is starting a new job.

   _____

6. You want to tell someone about a movie you have just seen.

   _____

7. You want to find out how much an item at a department store costs.

   _____

8. You have been invited to have lunch with a friend.

   _____

9. You are telling an interviewer about your last job.

   _____

10. You have a toothache.

    _____

D ▸ Check Up

Decide which end mark, if any, is needed for each sentence.

1. Help me
    A .   **B** ?   **C** !   **D** None

2. How many years have you taken piano lessons
    F .   **G** ?   **H** !   **J** None

3. How horrible this medicine tastes
    A .   **B** ?   **C** !   **D** None

4. I would like a cup of decaf coffee, please
    F .   **G** ?   **H** !   **J** None

Read each set of sentences. Choose the sentence that has the correct end mark.

5. **A** Keep your eyes on the road!

    B Water your plants twice a week?

    C When will the winners be announced.

    D The barber shop is closed on Monday!

6. **F** How spicy this sauce is.

    G Stop me if you've heard this one!

    H Can you solve the riddle?

    J The next museum tour starts in fifteen minutes!

7. **A** Fill out this form completely?

    B Elections will be held next Tuesday.

    C What kind of batteries does this camera use.

    D What a clever costume that is?

8. **F** Look both ways before you cross the street?

    G Our team won the championship!

    H This guitar needs to be tuned!

    J What a strange story that was?

9. **A** What a wonderful idea?

    B Do you have an account at the credit union.

    C The bridge is closed for repairs!

    D Don't feed the zoo animals.

10. **F** How funny that comic was?

    G What kind of car do you drive!

    H The repair shop gave me an estimate.

    J Do you have all the ingredients you need.

A ▸ Introduce

Commas: Compound Sentences and Introductory Words

Commas help to make sentences easier to understand. In compound sentences, commas are used to separate the two or more complete thoughts that make up the sentence. Each complete thought is expressed in an **independent clause** that contains a subject and a predicate. The conjunctions *and, or, nor, but, yet,* or *for* may connect two independent clauses. Place a comma after the first independent clause, before the conjunction.

> We searched <u>everywhere, but</u> we did not find the remote.

> Wait for me at the <u>clock, or</u> go home with Grandpa. (The understood *you* is the subject of each independent clause.)

No comma is needed if a sentence contains only a compound subject or a compound predicate.

> <u>Sandy and Helen</u> co-chaired the fund drive. (compound subject)

> Either <u>recycle or compost</u> those old newspapers. (compound predicate)

For each sentence, place commas wherever they are needed. Write *Correct* on the line if commas aren't needed.

1. Antonie attended school full-time and worked part-time. _____

2. We wanted to see the movie but all the tickets were sold. _____

3. I foolishly left my umbrella at the office and it rained all evening.

   _____

4. Samia often visits the outdoor market for it reminds her of her homeland.

   _____

5. Maurice collected and distributed a hundred food baskets. _____

6. Do you file your tax return early or do you wait for the deadline?

   _____

7. Joe is certified as a mechanic but he also does auto body work.

   _____

8. Neither the suitcase nor the duffle bag seemed suitable. _____

B ▶ Practice

At the beginning of sentences, commas follow some words and phrases.

Place a comma after *yes* or *no* if either word is used to answer a question or to make a comment.

> <u>No</u>, this seat is not available.

Place a comma after a long introductory phrase to separate it from the rest of the sentence.

> <u>Long before the alarm clock rang</u>, Patrick was wide awake.

Use a comma after a short introductory phrase only if the sentence is hard to understand without it.

> <u>For the last time</u>, I don't need any more insurance.
> <u>Before sunset</u> the last of the boaters had returned to the dock.

Underline the introductory word or phrase in each sentence. Insert a comma after the phrase if it is needed.

1. To raise money for his favorite charity Christopher organized a 10K race.

2. For one thing swampland is no place to build a beach house.

3. Yes I do have change for a dollar.

4. Swinging wildly Francis whacked the baseball out of the park.

5. After the frost my delicate plants looked rather wilted.

6. For that matter you've been working overtime all week.

Circle the letter of the sentence in each pair in which the comma is used correctly.

7. **A** Since it was, before nine o'clock the bank was not open.

   B Since it was before nine o'clock, the bank was not open.

8. **A** During the thunderstorm we sought shelter in the nearby shed.

   B During the thunderstorm, we sought shelter in the nearby shed.

9. **A** By the way, would you help me next Saturday?

   B By the way would you help me next Saturday?

10. **A** Yes, I've read today's newspaper.

    B Yes I've read today's newspaper.

C ▶ Apply

Change each given sentence to a compound sentence by adding a connecting word from the box and another independent clause. Place commas wherever they are needed.

and	or	nor	but	for	yet

1. We spent all day Saturday shopping for a new car.

   _____

   _____

2. Dolores hoped to spend more time with her grandchildren.

   _____

   _____

3. Would tomorrow be a good time to shop?

   _____

   _____

4. Neither side appeared ready to compromise.

   _____

   _____

In each sentence below, add commas wherever they are needed. Place an X on any comma that is unnecessary or incorrect. Write C on the line if the sentence is correct as it is.

5. Drop off the plans at the office today, or bring them with you tomorrow. _____

6. No Mrs. Brown does not live here anymore but I can give you her new address.

   _____

7. Everyone heard the dishes crash to the floor, and rushed to see what had

   happened. _____

8. Neither Aunt Frieda, nor Uncle Salvator seemed tired yet it was after midnight.

   _____

D Check Up

Read each paragraph and look at the numbered, underlined parts. Choose the answer that is written correctly for each underlined part.

(1)   One of the largest swamp areas in the <u>world the Everglades</u> are
(2) located in southern Florida. Sawgrass covers parts of the <u>area and,</u>
(3) various trees <u>grow and thrive</u> there as well. The region contains many
(4) <u>birds and reptiles for</u> the jungle-like area provides food and shelter.
Alligators and crocodiles are its most famous inhabitants.

1. **A** world the Everglades,
    B world, the Everglades,
    C world, the Everglades
    D Correct as it is

2. **F** area, and
    G area and
    H area, and,
    J Correct as it is

3. **A** grow, and, thrive
    B grow, and thrive
    C grow, and thrive,
    D Correct as it is

4. **F** birds, and reptiles for
    G birds and reptiles, for
    H birds, and reptiles, for
    J Correct as it is

(5)   Libraries contain thousands of <u>books, but</u> the modern library has more
(6) than that. While the printed word still fills the <u>stacks audio and visual</u>
materials vie for space as well. Computers are essential information tools.
(7) You can <u>read, or view, or listen</u> to just about anything. Why wait? Find the
(8) nearest <u>library, and prepare</u> to meet the world!

5. **A** books but
    B books, but,
    C books but,
    D Correct as it is

6. **F** stacks, audio, and visual
    G stacks audio, and, visual
    H stacks, audio and visual
    J Correct as it is

7. **A** read, or view or listen,
    B read or view or listen
    C read or view, or listen
    D Correct as it is

8. **F** library and, prepare
    G library, and, prepare
    H library and prepare
    J Correct as it is

Commas: Series and Parenthetical Expressions

If a sentence contains a series of three or more words or short phrases, use commas to separate the items. Add a comma after each word or phrase in the series except the last one.

> Mushrooms, olives, and peppers decorated the pizza.

> Nelson suffered a sprained ankle, two cracked ribs, and a bruised elbow when he slipped on the stairs.

If two or more adjectives are in a series, try saying the word *and* between each of the consecutive adjectives to see if it makes sense. If it does, add a comma between the adjectives. If it does not, leave the comma out.

> When are you going to get rid of that old, rattling, noisy car? (*Old and rattling and noisy* makes sense.)

> She wore a sparkling, glistening sapphire ring on her finger. (*Sparkling and glistening sapphire ring* makes sense; *sparkling and glistening and sapphire ring* does not.)

If the items are joined by a connecting word, no comma is necessary.

> The quilt has a pattern of squares and circles and hexagons.

Circle the letter of the sentence in each pair in which commas are used correctly.

1. **A** Plumbers, masons, and electricians are needed to build the stadium.

   B Plumbers, masons, and electricians, are needed to build the stadium.

2. **A** We caught a salmon, roasted it, and enjoyed its delicious flavor.

   B We caught a salmon, roasted it and, enjoyed its delicious flavor.

3. **A** Lois, and Pola, and Ashley are training to become financial analysts.

   B Lois and Pola and Ashley are training to become financial analysts.

4. **A** This rusty, wobbly, iron, bench should not be part of the seating arrangement.

   B This rusty, wobbly iron bench should not be part of the seating arrangement.

5. **A** Keep important records in a strong box, a safe, or a bank vault.

   B Keep important records in a strong box, a safe, or, a bank vault.

◆B◆ Practice

A sentence sometimes contains a word, phrase, or clause that adds emphasis, information, or a comment to the main idea. However, this added element could be dropped from the sentence without affecting its meaning. Such words are called **parenthetical expressions**. In most cases, commas are used both before and after a parenthetical expression to set it apart from the rest of the sentence.

> <u>Well,</u> this is just too expensive!
>
> We knew<u>, of course,</u> that Clarice would be interested.
>
> The composer of this piece<u>, most critics agree,</u> was Mozart.

Read each sentence and underline its parenthetical expression. Add commas wherever they are needed.

1. He decided however not to join us for dinner.

2. Oh did I say something I shouldn't have?

3. The citrus grove as the picture indicates lies just beyond the house.

4. Indeed that is the price for this nearly new truck.

5. Molly has a reason I suppose for skipping the organizational meeting.

6. Politicians generally speaking should consider their constituents.

7. Whatever his weaknesses are Lloyd is an excellent auditor.

8. The fall foliage will be colorful although very briefly in this area.

9. I'll choose a repair shop more carefully next time to be sure.

10. In conclusion we thank you for participating in our survey today.

11. Do intelligent people she wondered act that way?

12. Well maybe just a bit of chocolate cake won't add too many calories.

13. We could of course fly directly to Los Angeles and skip the layovers.

14. He would have come Arthur explained if he hadn't missed the bus.

C ▸ Apply

Read the following paragraph. Note the parts that are numbered and underlined. Choose the answer that is written correctly for each underlined part.

(1) A cauldron bubbles with hot <u>gases cinders and</u> molten lava. Suddenly
(2) the mass erupts. Rivers of lava <u>pour out, course downward, and</u> drop into
(3) the ocean. <u>As a matter of fact this</u> is a common occurrence in parts of the world.
(4) <u>Volcanoes indeed are</u> a spectacular reminder of our geological history.

1. **A** gases cinders, and
    B gases, cinders, and
    C gases, cinders, and,
    D Correct as it is

3. **A** As a matter of fact this,
    B As a matter, of fact this
    C As a matter of fact, this
    D Correct as it is

2. **F** pour out course downward and
    G pour, out, course, downward, and
    H pour out, course downward, and,
    J Correct as it is

4. **F** Volcanoes indeed are,
    G Volcanoes, indeed are
    H Volcanoes, indeed, are
    J Correct as it is

Rewrite all sentences that require commas. If the sentence does not need any commas, write *Correct* on the line.

5. Newspapers magazines and paperbacks filled the entire bookcase.

    _____

6. The price I guess is more than I can afford to pay.

    _____

7. Brad or his wife or their son could drive you to your appointment.

    _____

8. Dozens of unhappy dissatisfied impatient customers waited in the complaint line.

    _____

9. Do you know for instance the capitals of Oregon Montana or Missouri?

    _____

10. The bicycle hit a bump wobbled slightiy and slipped sideways.

    _____

D Check Up

Read each sentence and note the underlined part. Choose the answer that is written correctly for each underlined part.

1. The <u>problem as we heard today involves</u> more than just our business.

   A problem as we heard today, involves

   B problem, as we heard today involves

   C problem, as we heard today, involves

   D Correct as it is

2. Great swarms of <u>mosquitoes, flies and gnats</u> made the camping trip less than enjoyable.

   F mosquitoes, flies, and gnats

   G mosquitoes flies and gnats

   H mosquitoes, flies, and, gnats

   J Correct as it is

3. Dr. Sanchez is an <u>ear nose and throat</u> specialist.

   A ear, nose and throat

   B ear, nose, and throat

   C ear, nose, and throat,

   D Correct as it is

4. Myra's cat <u>was indeed an aloof, pampered independent</u> feline.

   F was indeed an aloof, pampered, independent

   G was, indeed, an aloof, pampered, independent

   H was, indeed, an aloof, pampered, independent,

   J Correct as it is

5. <u>Soon after Larry Elaine and I</u> will explain the new shipping regulations.

   A Soon after Larry, Elaine, and I

   B Soon after, Larry, Elaine, and I

   C Soon after, Larry, Elaine and I

   D Correct as it is

6. The group <u>sang to put it kindly</u> somewhat off-key.

   F sang to put it kindly,

   G sang, to put it, kindly

   H sang, to put it kindly,

   J Correct as it is

7. This table comes in <u>pine oak walnut, or cherry</u> finishes.

   A pine, oak, walnut, or cherry

   B pine, oak, walnut, or, cherry

   C pine, oak, walnut, or cherry,

   D Correct as it is

8. Our table was laden with <u>salads bowls of pasta garlic bread and jugs of soda.</u>

   F salads, bowls of pasta, garlic bread, and jugs of soda.

   G salads, bowls of pasta, garlic bread and, jugs of soda.

   H salads, bowls of pasta, garlic, bread, and jugs of soda.

   J Correct as it is

Other Uses of Commas

Commas set off the name of a person or thing directly addressed. In the following examples, notice where commas are placed when the words of direct address come at the beginning, end, or middle of a sentence.

> Mr. Morris, your table is ready for you now.
>
> Are you thinking of joining the service, Brittany?
>
> Come on, you rusted heap, or I'll drive you to the junkyard!

Put a comma between the names of a city and a state in a sentence. Put a second comma after the name of the state if the sentence continues.

> Many horse farms are located near Lexington, Kentucky.
>
> Did you grow up in Omaha, Nebraska, or here in Maine?

Read each sentence and add commas wherever they are needed.

1. Take Madison Avenue Bob and you will miss the traffic jam.

2. Tell me Felice are you planning to stop in San Diego California?

3. The letter is on your desk Mr. Fisk.

4. Here are the pictures of my trip to Albuquerque New Mexico Mom.

For each item, circle the letter of the sentence in which commas are used correctly.

5. A Judith were you planning to move to Portland, Maine or Portland, Oregon?

   B Judith, were you planning to move to Portland, Maine, or Portland, Oregon?

6. A Take my advice, Gilbert, and learn how to repair computers.

   B Take my advice, Gilbert and learn how to repair computers.

7. A Does this jacket come in a larger size, young man?

   B Does this jacket come in a larger size young man?

8. A Sorry pooch, I'm not taking you for a walk in this storm.

   B Sorry, pooch, I'm not taking you for a walk in this storm.

B ◆ Practice

A word or a phrase used to explain another word is called an **appositive.** Appositives name the same thing as the words they explain. In sentences, appositives must be set off with commas.

My older brother, Nicholas, is attending night school.

We stopped at the Sweet Tooth, a candy store, on the way home.

When an appositive is introduced with words such as *or* or *namely*, include such words within the commas.

A joey, or young kangaroo, spends several months in its mother's pouch.

Underline the appositive in each sentence. On the line, write the word (or words) explained by the appositive.

1. The Crab Shack, a sea food restaurant, is on Pier 11. _____

2. Bill and Helene, my neighbors, have been very helpful to me.

   _____

3. Deborah's father, a man of few words, loved to read. _____

4. Dale watches every game played by his favorite team, the Whales.

   _____

5. Each of us ate a hoecake, or a special corn bread, with our meal.

   _____

Read each sentence. Add commas wherever necessary.

6. Tony a popular barber enjoys talking sports with his customers.

7. Our favorite restaurant China Garden serves great egg rolls.

8. One of the custodians Miguel Olivera has been with the company ten years.

9. My daughter's skating club the Rolling Wheels meets every week.

10. Maria's home a brick colonial is near Lansing, Michigan.

11. Hundreds of fry or newly hatched fish darted around the small pond.

12. Columbus the capital of Ohio is in the central part of the state.

C Apply

Rewrite each of the following sentences, placing commas correctly.

1. The PTA president Ali Takla has requested more parental involvement.

   _____

2. Owen's job assistant zoo keeper reflected his deep love of animals.

   _____

3. Natasha took her car to the closest repair shop Al's Tire and Battery.

   _____

4. Ron's prized possession a battered guitar leaned against his chair.

   _____

5. One of my favorite bushes is the ilex or holly.

   _____

Read the directions for each item below. Write a sentence using the underlined word in direct address. Be sure to add all necessary punctuation.

6. Tell <u>Dr. Barry</u> about a health problem.

   _____

7. Ask your <u>brother</u> to drive you to work.

   _____

8. Give <u>Mrs. Smith</u> your telephone number.

   _____

9. Tell <u>Jim</u> what is wrong with your car.

   _____

10. Suggest a movie that <u>Sarah</u> might enjoy seeing.

    _____

11. Relate something that happened today to <u>Maurice</u>.

    _____

D Check Up

Read each group of sentences. Choose the sentence that is punctuated correctly.

1. A Is it true, Jim that you're moving to Boise, Idaho?

    B Ray Mason, a well-known lawyer, is handling the case.

    C Williamsburg, Virginia is a restored colonial town Samantha.

    D Bruce say hello to Mrs. Tuttle, the owner of our apartment building.

2. F The baseball team traveled from Baltimore, Maryland, to Sarasota, Florida.

    G Take Highway 1 to Carmel California, Elizabeth.

    H A piroque or canoe is made by hollowing out a tree trunk.

    J I've told you before Lydia, just call when you need a ride.

3. A Milan, Ohio is the birthplace of Thomas A. Edison inventor of the electric light.

    B Our good friend Josh Summerfelt is working in Honolulu, Hawaii.

    C Have you decided, Annette, to buy the house in that new development, Ashton Acres?

    D Dewey take a picture of, Martha, standing next to the monument.

4. F Philadelphia, the home of the Liberty Bell is in Pennsylvania.

    G Please bring us the bill waiter.

    H You can't miss the Towers, a tall brick building on your left.

    J Stay away from the campfire, son or you may get burned.

Read each sentence and look at the underlined part. Choose the answer that is written correctly for the underlined part.

5. Katharine Lee <u>Bates an American poet and educator,</u> wrote the words for "America the Beautiful."

    A Bates, an American poet and educator,

    B Bates, an American, poet and educator,

    C Bates an American poet and educator

    D Correct as it is

6. <u>Cheyenne, Wyoming, Stephen</u> is north of Denver, Colorado.

    F Cheyenne, Wyoming Stephen,

    G Cheyenne Wyoming, Stephen

    H Cheyenne, Wyoming, Stephen,

    J Correct as it is

A Introduce

Semicolons and Colons

Use a semicolon to join the independent clauses of a compound sentence instead of using a conjunction and a comma. (Do not use a semicolon after a dependent clause. Use a comma.)

Right: Snow was drifting over the mountain roads; officials closed the pass. (two independent clauses)

Wrong: Because snow was drifting over the mountain roads; officials closed the pass. (first clause is dependent)

Use a semicolon between clauses in a compound sentence in which an adverb or a transitional phrase joins the clauses. Place a semicolon before the adverb or transitional phrase and a comma after it.

Jamal knew that driving would be hazardous; nevertheless, he drove to work that morning.

Use a semicolon between items in a series if those items already contain commas.

Officials declared a state of emergency in Bismarck, North Dakota; Minneapolis, Minnesota; and Omaha, Nebraska.

Insert a semicolon in the correct place(s) in each sentence.

1. The wind was blowing hard however, the TV reporter's hair did not move at all.

2. The sale prices are good on small, medium, and large T-shirts red, green, and blue caps and all the refrigerator magnets.

3. The climbers started up the mountain early in the morning they reached the top by mid-afternoon.

4. The audience seemed bored by the speaker nevertheless, they applauded for him politely.

5. The parade was led by the first-place winner, Kathryn Lange the second-place winner, Erin Black and the third-place winner, Gina Knight.

6. The cafeteria food was barely edible even so, it was the only food available during the short lunch break.

7. Brad gets up at six o'clock he reads the paper thoroughly before going to work.

8. Valerie introduced us to Barb, her sister Chris, her brother and Gloria, her cousin.

9. I think I'm late for a meeting do you know what time it is?

Use a colon to introduce a list of items. A colon should not be used except after the words *these* or *the following.*

Right: There are openings for the following types of workers: secretaries, receptionists, and custodians.

Wrong: There are openings for: secretaries, receptionists, and custodians.

Use a colon between numerals that tell the hour and the minute.

I heard the explosion at exactly 9:32 A.M.

Read each sentence. Add semicolons or colons wherever necessary. Place an *X* over any semicolon or colon that is used incorrectly.

1. The garden was filled with: petunias, impatiens, daisies, and marigolds.

2. The bus leaves the station at exactly 814 A.M.

3. Sally's list of favorite rides at the amusement park included the following the Racing Coaster, the Flying Turns, and the Scrambler.

4. The cash machine is easy to use however, my grandparents prefer working with a teller inside the bank.

5. Bill found himself locked out suddenly, he remembered the extra key beneath the welcome mat by the back door.

For each item, circle the letter of the sentence that is punctuated correctly.

6. **A** The garden had been neglected, tall weeds grew: among the roses.

   B The garden had been neglected; tall weeds grew among the roses.

7. **A** Before she goes to bed at night, Jamie lays out her clothes for the next day.

   B Before she goes to bed at night; Jamie lays out her clothes for the next day.

8. **A** The doll was expensive; however, it was exactly what Wendy wanted for her birthday.

   B The doll was expensive however; it was exactly what Wendy wanted for her birthday.

9. **A** The Italian restaurant offered these dishes: lasagna, ravioli, and spaghetti.

   B The Italian restaurant offered these dishes lasagna, ravioli, and spaghetti.

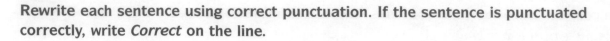

Rewrite each sentence using correct punctuation. If the sentence is punctuated correctly, write *Correct* on the line.

1. The following students: should report to the office; Jo Andrews, Pat Ryan, and Joe Lopez.

   _____

2. The book was good the movie was better.

   _____

3. Frank waited in the car with the engine running, finally; he turned it off.

   _____

4. You will find newspapers, magazines, and yearbooks in the reading room novels, biographies, and mysteries in the main room and picture books in the children's room.

   _____

5. Although the play started late; it ended exactly at 10;00 P.M.

   _____

6. Waves were high; and the small boat was taking in water.

   _____

7. Inez bought these gifts for her nephew: a rattle, a bib, and a sleeper.

   _____

8. Karen makes fancy meals for example, she cooked beef Wellington last night.

   _____

9. Greg has an interview at Kenner Industries; a company near the freeway.

   _____

10. On our vacation we went to: New York, New York, Portland, Maine, and Hartford, Connecticut.

    _____

D ▸ Check Up

Read each set of sentences. Choose the sentence that has correct use of semicolons and colons.

1. **A** The petting zoo has: goats, cats, and sheep.

   B I'll meet you at the restaurant at 8;00 P.M.

   C I have never visited the ocean; but I hope to see it someday.

   D It has stopped raining; in fact, the sun is shining brightly.

2. **F** Here are Ted, the drummer, Bob, the guitarist, and Isaac, the bass player.

   G The band is in town tonight; it is appearing at the music hall.

   H They have shows at 9'00 and at 10'30.

   J Tickets are hard to find now luckily, I bought mine days ago.

3. **A** I want to see these attractions in New York City: the Statue of Liberty, the Brooklyn Bridge, and the Empire State Building.

   B Would you rather have an apple pie; a cherry pie; or a peach pie?

   C While the orchestra is playing; no one may be seated.

   D The Turners are making plans; to remodel their kitchen.

4. **F** The elevator is broken; consequently, we'll have to use the stairs.

   G Even though the baby was crying; Hector slept soundly.

   H Don't forget these items; insect repellant, matches, and a cap.

   J Anne has a plan, she wants: to manage a day care center.

Read the paragraph and look at its numbered, underlined parts. Choose the answer that is written correctly for each underlined part.

The following kinds of columns are used in Greek buildings: the Doric, the
(5) Ionic, and the Corinthian. The Doric <u>column; the</u> simplest kind, is also
the oldest. The Ionic column is thinner and fancier than the Doric. All
(6) three columns are <u>attractive however,</u> it is the Corinthian that is the most
elaborate; it is decorated with carved leaves and flowers.

5. **A** column, the

   B column: the

   C column the

   D Correct as it is

6. **F** attractive, however;

   G attractive however;

   H attractive; however,

   J Correct as it is

Review

End Marks

All statements and most commands end with a period. A direct question requires a question mark. A sentence that expresses great excitement or emotion ends with an exclamation point. A command that expresses urgency or strong feeling also ends with an exclamation point.

Commas

Commas are used in the following instances:

- between independent clauses joined by a conjunction in a compound sentence. Conjunctions include *and, or, nor, but, yet* and *for*.
- after *yes* or *no* introducing a sentence. *Yes* or *no* must be used in response to a question or to make a comment.
- after certain short phrases and all long phrases that begin a sentence
- between words or phrases written in a series of three or more when no conjunctions join the items
- between parenthetical expressions and the rest of the sentence
- between the name of someone or something being directly addressed and the rest of the sentence
- between the name of a city and a state. Add a comma after the name of the state if the sentence continues.
- between an appositive and the rest of the sentence

Semicolons

Semicolons are used in these special situations:

- between independent clauses in a compound sentence if there is no conjunction
- after the first clause in a compound sentence if an adverb or a transitional phrase follows it. Place a comma after the adverb or transitional phrase.
- between items in a series, if those items contain commas

Colons

Colons have the following uses:

- introducing a list of items with *these* or *the following*
- separating numerals that name the hour and the minute

Decide which punctuation mark, if any, is needed in each sentence.

1. Thanks for your help Tim.
   A ;   B ,   C :   D None

2. The earthquake struck at 1058 P.M.
   F ,   G :   H ;   J None

3. Hurry with that fire extinguisher
   A ?   B .   C !   D None

4. Johnny ran in the marathon today he'll be sore tomorrow.
   F ,   G ;   H !   J None

5. Keep your gear on the back seat or store it in the trunk.
   A ,   B ;   C :   D None

6. The cafeteria looked crowded however, the snack bar had only a few customers.
   F ,   G .   H ;   J None

Read each sentence and look at the underlined part. Choose the answer that is written correctly for the underlined part.

7. Does this flight stop in <u>Orlando, Florida</u> before going on to San Juan?

   A Orlando Florida,

   B Orlando, Florida;

   C Orlando, Florida,

   D Correct as it is

8. The day was mild and <u>sunny, yet</u> Isabelle felt chilly.

   F sunny yet

   G sunny; yet

   H sunny, yet,

   J Correct as it is

9. After we finish <u>work Charlie</u> let's stop for a hamburger.

   A work. Charlie

   B work, Charlie,

   C work Charlie,

   D Correct as it is

10. The aquarium's diverse collection includes the following <u>species: mako, a type of shark;</u> neon goby, a tropical fish; and the moray eel, a fierce predator.

    F species, mako, a type of shark,

    G species; mako, a type of shark;

    H species: mako a type of shark,

    J Correct as it is

Read each set of sentences. Choose the sentence that is punctuated correctly.

11. A Ecru and cream and natural are very similar colors, Bernice.

   B This artifact as the curator pointed out is thousands of years old.

   C Go by subway, Lillie the bus takes too long.

   D We arrived at the airport an hour early, nevertheless, we missed our flight.

12. F Yes Alex Haley, the author of *Roots*, was born in Ithaca, New York.

   G The work was tedious yet Peter never complained.

   H Portia, are you sure about that.

   J Well, that's highly unlikely to happen.

13. A Laura was born and raised in Charleston West Virginia.

   B Does the lawn food contain: phosphorus, nitrogen, and potash?

   C Wow, what a tackle that was!

   D Oscar my son-in-law, is thirty years old today.

14. F Colin shoveled the snow in my driveway; I welcomed his help.

   G Last summer, we visited Mt. Whitney the highest mountain in California.

   H Yes the store is open evenings until 9:00 P.M.

   J Between the fence, and the alley, Stephano planted several large shrubs.

15. A Complaining loudly Cynthia took the trash to the curb.

   B Cold tired and hungry, Ramon finished work and drove home.

   C Emily, and her brother are renovating an old farmhouse?

   D Stop that chattering at once!

16. F Issac made an appetizer, cream of mushroom soup, a main entrée, roast beef and noodles, and a dessert, apple pie.

   G The eagle clutched a wriggling trout in its talon, or claw.

   H Although the auditorium was crowded Allison caught sight of us immediately.

   J No, Sabrina, doesn't work here anymore.

17. A Tanika felt a twinge in her ankle; even so, she continued walking.

   B At present, I'd be happy with say a 10 percent raise.

   C Albert is from Chattanooga, Tennessee and he often returns to visit.

   D The early news begins at 10:00 but tonight it was delayed 15 minutes.

Look at the numbered, underlined parts in each paragraph. Choose the correct answer for each underlined part.

What could be more delicious than homemade bread? Today's bread machines
(18) make short work of the task. Just pour in the liquid, usually <u>water or milk or juice</u>
(19) add dry ingredients, <u>like flour, sugar, salt, and yeast;</u> and set the dial for the
(20) required time. Within an <u>hour or two,</u> the fresh bread is baked. Remove the
(21) crusty loaf from the pan, slather on your favorite <u>spread and enjoy.</u>

18. **F** water, or milk, or juice

    G water, or milk, or juice,

    H water or milk or juice;

    J Correct as it is

20. **F** hour, or two,

    G hour, or, two

    H hour or, two,

    J Correct as it is

19. **A** like: flour, sugar, salt, and yeast

    B like flour, sugar, salt, and yeast,

    C like flour, sugar, salt and yeast,

    D Correct as it is

21. **A** spread, and enjoy!

    B spread and enjoy!

    C spread, and enjoy?

    D Correct as it is

(22)   The Winter <u>Olympics an international sports competition</u> is held every four
years. Exciting skiing, ice-skating, and ice hockey events tend to dominate the
(23) <u>Games but</u> bobsledding and luge competitions draw their share of fans, too.
Athletes compete for gold, silver, and bronze medals.

22. **F** Olympics, an international sports competition

    G Olympics an international sports competition,

    H Olympics, an international sports competition,

    J Correct as it is

23. **A** Games, but

    B Games; but,

    C Games but,

    D Correct as it is

Writing Quotations

A **direct quotation** is a speaker's exact words. When you repeat a speaker's words orally, your tone of voice and the pauses you use let listeners know that it is a direct quotation. When you write, you must use visual symbols to show you are quoting someone.

To write a direct quotation, enclose the speaker's words in quotation marks (" "). Place quotation marks around the words the speaker says, not the phrase that identifies the speaker. Always place the end mark for the quotation within the quotation marks, and capitalize the first word of a direct quotation.

> The flight attendant asked, "Do you need a blanket?"

An **indirect quotation** communicates a speaker's message but does not use his or her exact words. When you write an indirect quotation, do not use quotation marks.

> **Indirect:** The attendant told us to put our seat belts on.
> **Direct:** The attendant said, "Please put your seat belts on now."

Decide if each sentence is a direct quotation or an indirect quotation. Write _D_ or _I_ on the line. For each direct quotation, add quotation marks wherever they are needed.

1. _____ The bank teller said, Please endorse your check.

2. _____ What an amazing deal that was! exclaimed Liz.

3. _____ Heather said that she would be home late tonight.

4. _____ Tyler asked, Which department handles customer complaints?

5. _____ My parents say that they will give us their old dining room table.

6. _____ How often do you check your e-mail? asked Kendra.

7. _____ The astronomer announced, There has been an important discovery!

8. _____ Witnesses say that the damage from the tornado is incredible.

9. _____ This beach is always busy on summer weekends, said Hasan.

10. _____ My doctor predicted that I would feel better in about a week.

11. _____ Allie called to her friend, Hurry or you'll miss the bus!

12. _____ This VCR hasn't worked well since I bought it, the customer complained.

B Practice

Sometimes the phrase that identifies a speaker comes before the quotation. When that happens, place a comma after the phrase and before the quotation mark.

> The passenger asked, "When is the plane scheduled to land?"

In other sentences, the phrase that identifies the speaker comes after the quotation. If the quotation is a statement, use a comma instead of a period. Place the comma within the quotation marks. (Other end marks should be placed within the quotation marks, as usual.)

> "We will land in about ten minutes," the pilot said.

Occasionally, you may want to write a divided quotation in which the phrase that identifies the speaker interrupts the quotation. If so, enclose each part of the quotation in a set of quotation marks. Do not capitalize the second part of a divided quotation unless it begins a new sentence.

> "We are about to land," said the flight attendant, "so put your tray tables up."
> "I can't wait to land," said Quiana. "My family is waiting for me."

Read each sentence. Add commas wherever they are needed.

1. The governor said "We are proud of our record of accomplishment."

2. "Listen to my cell phone's ring" said Angela.

3. "My garden has been great" said James "but I am getting tired of zucchini."

4. Lamar shouted "I can't believe we finally won the championship!"

Read each of the following pairs of sentences. Circle the letter of the sentence that is capitalized and punctuated correctly.

5. A "I need to make a dental appointment for my son said Mary Ann."

   B "I need to make a dental appointment for my son," said Mary Ann.

6. A Meryl asked "who is picking Jerome up after school today"?

   B Meryl asked, "Who is picking Jerome up after school today?"

7. A "Does this job require a great deal of telephone work?" asked Kristen.

   B "Does this job require a great deal of telephone work," asked Kristen?

8. A "Workers have torn up the road," said Marcus, "so drive carefully."

   B "Workers have torn up the road" said Marcus, "So drive carefully."

C ▸ Apply

Rewrite each sentence correctly on the line. If it is capitalized and punctuated correctly, write *Correct* on the line.

1. "Adam said let's paint this room green."

   _____

2. The magazine writer said to stay with neutral colors.

   _____

3. "Is green a neutral color," asked Roz.

   _____

4. "It may not be neutral." said Adam, "But I'm tired of white walls."

   _____

5. Roz admitted; "I think I'm ready for a change".

   _____

6. I just love the room's new look"! exclaimed Roz.

   _____

7. "Which room should we paint next?" asked Adam.

   _____

Choose one of the topics below and circle it. Then follow the directions beside the item numbers to write quotations about that topic. Be sure to capitalize and punctuate the quotations correctly.

weather   careers   entertainment   family life

8. Write a question that is a direct quotation.

   _____

9. Write an indirect quotation.

   _____

10. Write a direct quotation that is interrupted by a phrase identifying the speaker.

    _____

D ▶ Check Up

For each item, choose the answer that is written correctly for the underlined part.

1. The vet asked <u>me, to</u> hold my dog while she gave it a shot.

   A me, "to

   B me to

   C "me to,

   D Correct as it is

2. <u>"my advice</u> is to pay off your credit card," said the financial advisor.

   F "My advice

   G my advice

   H "My advice,"

   J Correct as it is

3. The minister asked, "Will you take this man to be your <u>husband"?</u>

   A husband?"

   B husband?

   C husband"?"

   D Correct as it is

4. The ranger <u>warned, "We</u> must all work together to preserve our environment."

   F warned, "we

   G warned "We

   H warned; "We

   J Correct as it is

Read each set of sentences below. Choose the sentence that is written correctly.

5. A Clay said, "don't forget to ask for a receipt."

   B "This trick, said the magician. Will astound you."

   C "Who would like to play some pinochle"? asked Margaret.

   D Steve said, "The salesman gave me a good deal on my new car."

6. F "Leave me alone," screamed the independent toddler!

   G "The washer ate one of my socks again" shouted Brad angrily.

   H Henry said that we should meet him in front of the theater.

   J The lifeguard told, "the children to stop their rough play."

7. A Lydia said; "I will make a decision very soon."

   B "Who brought the peach pie"? asked Sharon. "it's delicious."

   C "My car isn't pretty," said Cliff, "but it runs well."

   D "The boss said," Thank you all for a job well done.

8. F "I have one dog, one cat, and a parakeet." said Andy.

   G "What can I make you for breakfast?" asked Alana.

   H The salesclerk said, "Let me show you that style in black.

   J "I hope to find an antique dresser for my bedroom", said Jan.

Using the Apostrophe: Writing Contractions

In informal conversations, many people find it easier and quicker
to say a contraction than to pronounce two separate words. A
contraction is a word that joins two words and leaves out one
or more letters. When you write a contraction, an apostrophe
(') stands for the letters that were left out. Some contractions
are formed by combining a pronoun and a verb, as in the following examples:

he + is = he's	they + are = they're
she + is = she's	we + are = we're
it + is = it's	we + will = we'll
I + am = I'm	what + is = what's
I + have = I've	you + will = you'll

Other contractions combine a helping verb and the word *not*. The apostrophe replaces
the letters *no* or *o*. One contraction that is formed in an unusual way is *won't*, which
means "will not."

can + not = can't	have + not = haven't
could + not = couldn't	was + not = wasn't
did + not = didn't	were + not = weren't
has + not = hasn't	should + not = shouldn't

Two particularly troublesome contractions are *it's* and *they're*. They are often confused
with the possessive pronouns *its* and *their*. The apostrophe is used only with the
contractions, not with the possessive pronouns. If you are in doubt about whether to
use the contraction, mentally substitute the phrase *it is* or *they are* in the sentence. If the
sentence still makes sense, use the contraction.

> **Contraction:** It's dark in a cave. <u>They're</u> afraid of the dark.
> **Possessive pronoun:** I see <u>its</u> entrance. They need <u>their</u> lights.

**Underline the contraction in each sentence. On the lines, write the two words that
were joined to make the contraction.**

1. _____ + _____ The reporter hasn't interviewed the winner's family yet.

2. _____ + _____ It's difficult to estimate how long these trips will take.

3. _____ + _____ You shouldn't enter a cave without reliable light sources.

4. _____ + _____ Mountain climbing isn't Matthew's favorite sport.

5. _____ + _____ Maria tried hard, but she couldn't beat Joe's time.

B Practice

Read each of the following pairs of sentences. Circle the letter of the sentence in which the contraction is written correctly.

1. **A** Sylvia hopes that shel'l be elected president of her club.

   B Sylvia hopes that she'll be elected president of her club.

2. **A** It's late, and we should be getting back to my brother's house.

   B Its late, and we should be getting back to my brother's house.

3. **A** I'm still tired because I havent had my morning coffee yet.

   B I'm still tired because I haven't had my morning coffee yet.

4. **A** There's a white truck parked in your driveway.

   B Theirs a white truck parked in you're driveway.

5. **A** We're waiting for the committee's approval before we go ahead with the project.

   B Wer'e waiting for the committee's approval before we go ahead with the project.

6. **A** I'v'e applied at several hospital's as part of my current job search.

   B I've applied at several hospitals as part of my current job search.

Complete each sentence by circling the correct word in parentheses.

7. The newspaper ran (its, it's) headline in extra-large letters.

8. These phones are inexpensive, but (they're, their) extremely reliable.

9. (Its, It's) unfair to ask Regina to baby-sit every Saturday night.

10. In (their, they're) opinion, the mayor is doing an excellent job.

11. The trainees report that (they're, their) eager to begin their new jobs.

12. Some people think this show is hilarious, but I think (it's, its) just silly.

13. The officer who nabbed the robbers is sure that (their, they're) responsible for all the recent break-ins.

14. Place the cartons (there, they're) until we decide what to do with them.

15. It seems like (its, it's) always raining on the weekends lately.

16. This restaurant is known for (it's, its) delicious seafood dishes.

In each sentence, underline two words that can be joined in a contraction. On the line, write the contraction.

1. I was not aware that anyone had problems with the schedule.

   _____

2. Even though it is raining, I can see the sun shining. _____

3. Patrons without valid identification will not be admitted. _____

4. The explorers were not able to find the fabled Fountain of Youth.

   _____

5. After the game, we will have a party at Alex's house. _____

6. If you are serious about wanting this job, you must get a haircut.

   _____

Read the following paragraph. On each numbered line of text, circle a contraction that has been formed incorrectly. Then write it correctly on the corresponding line below.

(7)   Come one, come all to the closing sale of Dillon's Furniture. Yes, wer'e
(8) closing our doors forever. Weve' been in business for over ten years. At our
(9) local store, youl'l find deals that you have never seen before and that you may
(10) never see again. Did you say that you ca'nt find a living room set that you can
(11) afford? Then clearly yo'uve never seen our magnificent selection. And just look
(12) at the prices on our bedrooms! Our manager says that shes' been empowered
(13) to cut a deal with any credit-worthy customer. Its not too late to get an incredible
(14) bargain. But hurry! Lock in these savings before the'ir gone forever!

7. _____

8. _____

9. _____

10. _____

11. _____

12. _____

13. _____

14. _____

D Check Up

Read each set of sentences. Choose the sentence in which the contraction is written correctly.

1. **A** Gail had'nt been on vacation for long before she got homesick.
   B Whats' so great about sitting around with nothing to do?
   C She couldnt wait to resume work on her pet project.
   D Staff members weren't used to working without supervision.

2. **F** It's going to be hard to keep from laughing at this meeting.
   G Shoul'dnt we be decorating for the party tonight?
   H Their power went out last night, so there going to be late.
   J Even though Cheryl and Sharon are twins, their very different.

3. **A** If were late, start without us.
   B Because Ward is now vice president, he'll be president next year.
   C It seems that your'e pretty sure you can buy a ticket at the gate.
   D Charlie doe'snt go to the movies much anymore since he bought his DVD player.

4. **F** Wo'nt your mother be worried if you don't come home for dinner?
   G When your boss cant' remember your name, its time to look for a new job.
   H I'm anxious to learn how to use my new camera.
   J Jennie did'nt register for classes.

Read each sentence and look at the underlined word. Choose the answer that is written correctly for the underlined word.

5. Ask Sara if <u>she'll</u> be coming to the annual club luncheon.
   A shel'l
   B sh'ell
   C shell'
   D Correct as it is

6. My car needs some repairs. The mechanic said <u>its</u> brakes must be replaced.
   F it's
   G its'
   H it's'
   J Correct as it is

7. <u>Could'nt</u> you arrange your schedule so you are free for dinner tonight?
   A Could'n't
   B Coul'd'nt
   C Couldn't
   D Correct as it is

8. Whenever <u>your</u> out of the house, your dog sits on your bed.
   F you'r
   G you're
   H your'e
   J Correct as it is

Using the Apostrophe: Writing Possessive Nouns

A **possessive noun** shows possession or ownership of the noun that follows it. Every time you write a possessive noun, you must use an apostrophe ('). Follow these rules when you write possessive nouns:

- If the noun that names the owner is singular, add an apostrophe and the letter s.

  James's backpack   the pilot's uniform

- If the noun that names the owners is plural and ends in s, just add an apostrophe to the end of the word.

  the attendants' names   the friends' addresses

- If the noun that names the owners is plural but does not end in s, add an apostrophe and an s.

  mice's tails   women's interests

Apostrophes are used in possessive nouns and in contractions. Apostrophes are not used in the plural form of a noun.

Right: I forgot my tickets.   **Wrong:** I forgot my ticket's.

Write a phrase that has the same meaning as the given phrase but uses a possessive noun. Be sure to insert the apostrophe in the correct place.

   Example: the songs of the birds

   the birds' songs

1. the tools that belong to the workers _____

2. the aides of the senator _____

3. the diplomas that belong to the graduates _____

4. the smile that Myra has _____

5. the cave of the bear _____

6. the flight path of the geese _____

7. the tests that belong to the students _____

8. the decoys that belong to the hunters _____

9. the tennis match of the men _____

B Practice

Remember not to use an apostrophe in the possessive form of personal pronouns. The following are personal pronouns:

> his   hers   its   ours   yours   theirs

For each item, circle the letter of the sentence in which apostrophes are used correctly.

1. **A** Is this Shontae's handbag or yours?

   B Is this Shontaes handbag or your's?

2. **A** All of these fruit tree's were planted by Josephs' grandfather.

   B All of these fruit trees were planted by Joseph's grandfather.

3. **A** One employees' lunch has been in the office refrigerator for two weeks.

   B One employee's lunch has been in the office refrigerator for two weeks.

4. **A** This fence should stop the Goddards' cats from sneaking into our yard.

   B This fence should stop the Goddard's cat's from sneaking into our yard.

5. **A** My mother's line was busy after breakfast, so I called her later in the day.

   B My mothers' line was busy after breakfast, so I called her later in the day.

Each of the following sentences has a possessive that is written incorrectly. Underline the possessive. Then write it correctly on the line.

6. I remember playing in the Gordons backyard as a child.

   _____

7. Someone put a glass of water in the speakers' hand; she took a drink and continued.

   _____

8. It is Christies hope that she'll be back home again in about a month.

   _____

9. We wanted to shake the actor's hands, but they left right after the play.

   _____

10. The conductor tapped his baton to get all the musician's' attention.

   _____

C ▶ Apply

Read each of the following sentences. If the sentence is not written correctly, rewrite it correctly on the line. If it is written correctly, write *Correct* on the line.

1. Richs dog is gentle, but it's bark can sound vicious.

   _____

2. We're anxious to hear all about Florence's new job.

   _____

3. It is the Browns contention that the fault cannot be their's.

   _____

4. Children's stories are often not as simple as they seem.

   _____

5. The congressmans' Web site posts his stand on the issues'.

   _____

Underline a phrase in each of the following sentences that can be changed to include a possessive. On the line, write a new sentence using that possessive.

   Example: The <u>haircut of Victor</u> makes him look younger.
   Have you seen <u>Victor's haircut</u>?

6. A recent poll revealed the opinions of the voters regarding the state lottery.

   _____

7. The toys that belong to the children are scattered all over the floor.

   _____

8. Auditors carefully reviewed the budget of the organization.

   _____

9. I'm afraid the home of the skunks is under our porch.

   _____

10. The energy that belonged to the runners faded as the hours went by.

   _____

D Check Up

Read each set of sentences. Choose the sentence that is written correctly.

1. **A** Lesley's lawyer has advised her not to talk to the press.

   B I can't believe the winning ticket is our's!

   C The painters easel fell down when his dog brushed against it.

   D Many museum patrons' enjoy the special monthly displays.

2. **F** The river flowed over it's banks and flooded the city.

   G If Jennifer wants it, the job is her's.

   H Viewers' reactions to the documentary were mixed.

   J The childrens parents sat on the nearby park benches.

3. **A** No one could break through the strikers picket line's.

   B During the argument, the men's voices became loud and angry.

   C Maybe Derek can borrow a mechanics' tools to finish the job.

   D All my aunt's and uncle's came to my parents anniversary party.

4. **F** Our chicken wing's are spicier than their's.

   G The horse seemed glad to get back into it's stall after the ride.

   H I always forget that jokes' punchline.

   J Michael's sense of humor is a little offbeat.

Read each sentence and look at the underlined word. Choose the answer that is written correctly for the underlined word.

5. Many <u>critics</u> reviews have praised the play that just opened at the playhouse.

   A critics'

   B critic's

   C critic's'

   D Correct as it is

6. Whenever <u>Jasons'</u> team takes the field, everyone cheers.

   F Jasons

   G Jason's

   H Jason's'

   J Correct as it is

7. Is a <u>farmer's</u> busiest time in the spring or in the fall?

   A farmers

   B farmers'

   C farmer's'

   D Correct as it is

8. The <u>callers</u> phone was cheap, and it distorted his voice.

   F caller's

   G callers'

   H caller's'

   J Correct as it is

Writing Business Letters

Businesses depend on clear communication with customers and clients. Most business letters use the widely accepted format shown below.

The **heading** is the date on which the letter is written. Insert a comma between the day of the month and the year.

The **inside address** is the recipient's address. It usually has three lines: the name of the individual or business; the street address or post office box; and the city, state, and ZIP code. Capitalize all proper nouns and their abbreviations in the inside address. Remember that any abbreviation in the address must be followed by a period. Insert a comma between the names of the city and the state. No comma is needed between the state and the ZIP code.

The **salutation,** also called the **greeting,** is like the "hello" in a conversation. The salutation usually begins with the capitalized word *Dear* and always ends with a colon. The recipient's name is capitalized. If you don't know the name of the recipient, you may use a general greeting such as *Dear Sir or Madam* or *To Whom It May Concern.*

The **body,** the writer's message, comes after the salutation. The first line of each paragraph is indented. The **closing,** which is the letter's "good-bye," follows the body. Only the first word of the closing is capitalized. The closing ends with a comma. The last letter part is the writer's **signature,** which is followed by his or her clearly printed name.

(Heading)	April 8, 2004
(Inside Address)	Brothers Painting Company
	3758 Lexington Ave.
	St. Louis, Missouri 63103
(Salutation)	Dear Sir or Madam:
(Body)	Enclosed please find a check to pay the final installment of my bill.
(Closing)	Yours truly,
(Signature)	*Renata Edwards*
	Renata Edwards

Each of the following letter parts contains one or more errors. Rewrite it correctly on the line.

1. july, 10 2004 _____

2. 1634 superior ave _____

3. ogden utah 84401 _____

4. dear dr. lee; _____

5. Dear sir, _____

6. very truly yours: _____

B Practice

The following letter parts are out of order. Most have capitalization or punctuation errors. Using the letter format shown on the previous page, write each letter part correctly in its proper place in the letter form below.

300 Shore rd.   Dear Sir Or Madam,

milwaukee Wisconsin: 53202   Elena Ruiz

wisconsin weekends, Inc   march, 15, 2005

sincerely Yours;   *Elena Ruiz*

I am planning a trip to Milwaukee Wisconsin with my family this summer. Please send me information about attractions that might appeal to my daughters, ages five and seven. Thank you in advance for your help.

Apply

Write a business letter on the lines below. Give the letter today's date. Use the following information: The recipient is Just Right Outfitters, located at 1514 Walnut St. in Portland, Oregon. Its ZIP code is 97205. Tell whoever gets the letter that you purchased a shirt after seeing its picture in a catalog. Explain that the shirt does not match the picture in the catalog, and you are returning it for a full refund. Be sure to capitalize and punctuate the letter correctly.

_____

_____

_____

_____

_____

_____

_____

_____

_____

_____

_____

_____

_____

_____

D Check Up

Read the following letter and note its numbered, underlined parts. Choose the answer that is written correctly for each underlined part.

(1) october 19, 2005

City Day Care

(2) 3435 Burlington blvd

(3) Dallas, texas, 75201

(4) Dear ms. Martin;

    I am seeking a position as a preschool caregiver. Having recently earned a certificate in Early Childhood Care from the local community college, I feel I am well qualified in the field. I am anxious to put my child care skills to work in the Dallas area. I am enclosing my résumé for your review. Please consider me for any openings at your center.

(5) Yours truly,

Monique Jimmison

Monique Jimmison

1. A October 19, 2005
   B October, 19, 2005
   C october, 19, 2005
   D Correct as it is

2. F 3435 burlington blvd.
   G 3435 Burlington Blvd.
   H 3435, burlington Blvd.
   J Correct as it is

3. A dallas, texas 75201
   B Dallas, Texas 75201
   C Dallas Texas, 75201
   D Correct as it is

4. F dear ms. martin:
   G Dear ms. Martin,
   H Dear Ms. Martin:
   J Correct as it is

5. A yours truly;
   B Yours truly:
   C Yours Truly,
   D Correct as it is

Review

UNIT 6

Writing Quotations

A **direct quotation** is a speaker's exact words. Pay special attention to the placement of quotation marks, commas, end marks, and the capitalization of first words in the examples below.

> "Have you read this article?" Paulina asked. "It's about furnaces."
>
> "I guess I should read it," said Matt, "since it's almost winter."

An **indirect quotation** communicates a speaker's message without using his or her exact words. No quotation marks are needed.

> Paulina told Matt that the article was about caring for furnaces.

Writing Contractions

A **contraction** combines two words but replaces one or more letters with an apostrophe. Contractions are formed by combining either a pronoun and a verb or a verb and *not*. Do not confuse the possessive pronouns *its* and *their* with the contractions *it's* and *they're*.

> they + are = they're   could + not = couldn't

Writing Possessive Nouns

To indicate ownership, add an apostrophe and *s* after a singular noun or after a plural noun that does not end in *s*. Add an apostrophe after a plural noun that ends in *s*. Plural nouns do not use an apostrophe.

> bird's wing   girls' desks   men's team

Writing a Business Letter

Note the capitalization and punctuation in the business letter below.

(Heading)   August 18, 2005

(Inside Address)   Homes for Today Magazine
                        13547 Martin Blvd.
                        Chicago, Illinois 60610

(Salutation)   Dear Sir or Madam:

(Body)   My address has changed. Please update your records.

(Closing)   Your subscriber,

(Signature)   Crystal Boynton

(Name)   Crystal Boynton

Read each set of sentences. Choose the sentence that is written correctly.

1. **A** "The new book store is opening on Saturday" said Barb.

   B Darrell wondered, "will they have any grand opening sale"

   C "I'm looking for a good cookbook," said Sue, "with recipes for vegetarian meals."

   D Anne said, "I need a good book to read before I go to sleep"?

2. **F** The babys' bib fell to the floor.

   G For my mothers' birthday, I bought her an exotic houseplant.

   H Adam coaches his sons softball team.

   J Gina's oldest son started school in September.

3. **A** The auctioneer said that the statue was over 100 years old.

   B The clerk said, "that it was time for her break."

   C "The saleswoman says that I can return the product if I'm not satisfied.

   D The receptionist told me that, "Mr. Ingram was out, but I could come back later."

4. **F** The children want to stay up late even though their tired.

   G I haven't read the book yet, but it's already overdue.

   H This tree loses it's leaves in early December.

   J Its a mystery how bird's know when to fly south.

5. **A** The guests have'nt arrived yet, but they'l be here soon.

   B I have written down the phone number were' supposed to call.

   C The magicians' last trick was his best.

   D "You've grown so tall, young lady," Grandma said.

6. **F** I hope that someone finds Audreys' dog today.

   G The secretary recorded the board member's votes for the minute's.

   H All the writers' names were listed at the front of the book.

   J All the neighbor's agree that the Ferguson's house needs painting.

7. **A** "I'm ordering a burger." said Ted. "you can order anything you want."

   B "All I know," complained Carla, "is that you are always late."

   C "Wait a minute" replied the secretary. I think she just got off the phone."

   D "The voters have spoken", said the defeated candidate.

8. **F** The pilot announced that the plane would land on time.

   G "The professor said that" the papers were due in two weeks.

   H "The nurse told me to fill out these forms." said Stanley.

   J The speaker explained that "she had been delayed at the airport."

Read the letters and the paragraph and look at the numbered, underlined parts. Choose the answer that is written correctly for each underlined part.

(9) <u>January 14 2005</u>

Miller's Audio

(10) <u>2156 washington blvd.</u>

(11) <u>Memphis, tennessee, 38103</u>

(12) <u>Dear Sir Or Madam,</u>

     I recently bought a CD player at your store, but I am sending it

(13) back. <u>Its</u> been giving me trouble ever since I got it home. It skips tracks on every compact disk. Sometimes it doesn't even recognize that a disk has been inserted. Since the player is under warranty, I am requesting that you either have it repaired or replace it.

(14) <u>Your Customer:</u>
    Steven Grant
    Steven Grant

9. A January, 14 2005

   B january, 14, 2005

   C January 14, 2005

   D Correct as it is

10. F 2156 Washington Blvd

   G 2156 Washington Blvd.

   H 2156 Washington blvd.

   J Correct as it is

11. A Memphis, Tennessee 38103

   B memphis, tennessee 38103

   C Memphis Tennessee: 38103

   D Correct as it is

12. F Dear Sir Or Madam:

   G Dear Sir or Madam:

   H dear sir or madam,

   J Correct as it is

13. A Its'

   B It's'

   C It's

   D Correct as it is

14. F Your customer:

   G Your Customer,

   H Your customer,

   J Correct as it is

March 22, 2004

On the Spot Employment Agency
1457 Second St.
Charlotte, North Carolina 28202

(15) <u>dear Ms. Campbell</u>

Thank you for taking the time to interview me yesterday.
After hearing how to present myself to a prospective employer, I feel more confident about my chances of getting a good job. Please contact me if you hear about any position that matches my skills.

(16) <u>Sincerely Yours,</u>
Akil Edwards
Akil Edwards

15. A dear Ms. Campbell,

B Dear Ms. Campbell:

C Dear Ms. campbell;

D Correct as it is

17. F Sincerely yours,

G Sincerely yours:

H sincerely yours:

J Correct as it is

(17)   An old saying <u>says, "A fool</u> and his money are soon parted." If you study the buying patterns of millions of Americans, you may agree with that
(18) saying. Many of us do seem foolish about money, buying items we <u>do'nt</u>
(19) really need. If you're wise, you'll consider your <u>familys</u> needs, as opposed to their wants. The money you save will come in handy when your sons or
(20) daughters want to go to college. <u>Theyl'l</u> thank you.

17. A says "A fool

B says "a fool

C says, A fool

D Correct as it is

19. A family's

B familys'

C famili'es

D Correct as it is

18. F dont'

G dont

H don't

J Correct as it is

20. F Thell

G They'll

H Theyll'

J Correct as it is

◆ Posttest

Decide which punctuation mark, if any, is needed in each sentence.

1. I would not want to be in Johns shoes for a million dollars.
   A '   B :   C "   D None

2. Enthusiastically, the salesperson said, "We have the best deals in town"
   F ,   G !   H ?   J None

3. I'm pleased to introduce my father Dr. Philip Day.
   A :   B ;   C ,   D None

4. The little shop sells kaleidoscopes books about scopes, and kits for making scopes.
   F ,   G :   H .   J None

5. "If you have any questions" said the teacher, "please raise your hand now."
   A "   B ,   C ;   D None

Choose the word or phrase that best completes each sentence.

6. Alex and Gloria _____ dogs for police work before they retired.

   F has trained

   G had trained

   H train

   J will have trained

7. In those days, people believed that the sun _____ stop shining.

   A would never

   B wouldn't never

   C would never hardly

   D wouldn't hardly ever

8. Before every game, the quarterback gave _____ a personal pep talk.

   F hisself

   G themselves

   H him

   J himself

9. It's easy to see why this model is the _____ house in the development.

   A expensivest

   B more expensive

   C most expensive

   D most expensivest

Read each set of sentences. Then choose the sentence that is written correctly and has correct capitalization and punctuation.

10. F After the temperature falls to 68°F, the furnace switched on.

    G I will clean the basement before the repairman came.

    H He says the furnace will need a checkup soon.

    J When the part was ordered, someone is making a mistake.

11. A Everyone accept Rich was here.

    B He must of overslept.

    C He would of come if anyone had remembered to remind him.

    D Should we accept his excuse?

12. F Many countries of Europe have adopted one currency, the euro.

    G Gone are the lira of italy and the mark of germany!

    H The European union began its move to the euro in 1998.

    J Crossing the english channel, you switch from euros to pounds.

13. A A list of the phone numbers a person uses regularly.

    B The speed-dial buttons on a telephone are useful.

    C Most phones have redial buttons those save a lot of effort.

    D we think cell phones are great!

14. F Rhonda said "that she hadn't slept at all the night before."

    G Do you often have insomnia?" Josef asked.

    H "When I can't sleep," Mort reported, "I drink some milk."

    J Caren said, "my problem is falling asleep too early!"

15. A Wev'e been looking for Nancy.

    B She should hear our guests reaction to the pie she brought.

    C I cant imagine anything tastier!

    D Won't you share your recipe?

16. F Ed and Naomi treated theirselves to a trip to Montana.

    G Later, both of them discussed his favorite experiences.

    H Certainly, the rodeo left its mark on their memories.

    J Each of the bucking broncos threw their riders within seconds.

17. A Cher, where are mufflers stored?

    B Headlights, our best-selling item are in the shelves on the right.

    C We order tires from Akron Ohio.

    D Wiper blades I believe are in the back room.

Read each set of underlined sentences. Then choose the sentence that best combines the underlined sentences.

18. Lois watched a diver feed fish at the aquarium.
Haruku watched a diver feed fish at the aquarium.

   F Lois watched a diver feed fish because Haruku watched a diver feed fish at the aquarium.

   G Lois watched a diver feed fish and so did Haruku at the aquarium.

   H Lois watched and Haruku watched the diver who fed fish at the aquarium.

   J Lois and Haruku watched a diver feed fish at the aquarium.

19. Angrily, Edward tried to scrape off some gum.
The gum was stuck to his shoe.

   A Angrily, Edward tried to scrape off some gum, and the gum was stuck to his shoe.

   B Angry and stuck to his shoe, Edward tried to scrape off some gum.

   C Edward, who was angry, tried to scrape off his shoe, but the gum was stuck on his shoe.

   D Angrily, Edward tried to scrape off some gum stuck to his shoe.

20. The CD of folk songs was good.
Emily listened to the CD last night.

   F The CD of folk songs was good, but Emily listened to the CD last night.

   G The CD of folk songs that Emily listened to last night was good.

   H The CD that Emily listened to of folk songs last night was good.

   J Although Emily listened to the CD of folk songs last night, the CD was good.

21. Arnold took a course on business franchises.
Later he bought a franchise.
He opened a doughnut shop.

   A After Arnold took a course on business franchises, he bought a franchise and opened a doughnut shop.

   B Arnold took a course that was on business franchises, and later he bought a franchise, and he opened a doughnut shop.

   C Arnold, who took a course on business franchises later, bought a franchise but opened a doughnut shop.

   D Although Arnold took a course on business franchises, he bought a franchise and later opened a doughnut shop.

Read each paragraph. Then choose the sentence that best fills the blank.

22.	My five-year-old daughter has developed an unusual way of eating cereal. First she pours the cereal into her bowl. She then mashes the dry cereal into crumbs. _____. She waits about ten minutes for the milk to be absorbed. Finally she sprinkles sugar over the cereal mush and eats it.

F	Neither of my sons plays with his cereal this way.

G	She doesn't like hot cereal much.

H	Next she pours milk over the cereal crumbs.

J	Next she chooses which cereal to eat that day.

23.	In one production of the opera Tosca, the leading lady was so unpleasant that the stage crew played a joke on her. In the final scene, the character Tosca commits suicide by jumping from a castle window. The singer was supposed to jump onto mattresses hidden behind the scenery. _____. The singer sang her last note and jumped. When she hit the trampoline, she bounced above the castle wall— again and again! Rather than crying for the character's tragic death, the audience laughed at the singer's predicament.

A	Furthermore, the stage crew put a trampoline there.

B	Consequently, the stage crew put a trampoline there.

C	Finally, the stage crew put a trampoline there.

D	Instead, the stage crew put a trampoline there.

24.	At the top of my closet is a dusty box holding a partially assembled dress. I chose the pattern and cut the cloth two years ago, before styles changed. When I started to sew the pieces together, the thread jammed my sewing machine, and I stopped work. Since then I've gained weight, and I no longer fit in that size. _____.

F	Sewing is a practical hobby that offers a chance for creativity as well.

G	It's beginning to look as if that dress will never be completed.

H	I used a striped cotton cloth for the dress.

J	Have you sewn any of your own clothes?

25.   Raccoons may look like cute masked robbers, but there's nothing cute about their behavior inside a house. One day my neighbor heard a noise in her living room. _____. In the fireplace were two raccoons who had fallen down the chimney. They caught their breath and began running around the room. Before my neighbor got them out of the house, her furniture and carpet were dirty and torn.

   A The raccoons were small and appealing.

   B Later she told us what happened.

   C She went to investigate.

   D She was upstairs in her bedroom.

Read each topic sentence. Then choose the answer that best develops the topic sentence.

26. Aquaculture, or raising crops in water, is gaining importance in the United States.

   F Around the world, water farmers raise both freshwater and saltwater fish. Some fish are raised in tanks, others in ponds, and still others in the ocean, enclosed in cages.

   G Although raising animals in water is more popular than raising plants, this second kind of aquaculture is still important. For example, seaweed is grown in many Asian countries for food and for use in paint, fertilizer, and other products.

   H At least twenty U.S. colleges or universities now offer degrees in aquaculture. Most of the graduates are going into fish farming, so that is growing more common. The number of fish farms in Utah, for example, jumped from zero in 1985 to eighteen just ten years later.

   J In Asia, many rice fields become fish farms during the rainy season when the fields flood. Farmers fill the fields with young fish and harvest them three months later when they have grown to full size.

27. Hurrying to pick up her son from day care, Liz ran into serious gridlock.

   A As the number of working moms increases, the need for reliable day care also increases. Some companies provide day care centers within their office buildings.

   B The term *gridlock* is an Americanism, a term that began in, or is used only in, America. Many Americanisms have made their way into the English language.

   C Liz and her husband shared the job of picking up Leland. This was Tuesday, one of Liz's days.

   D The first heavy snowfall of the season had started early that afternoon, resulting in a larger number of fender-bender accidents than usual. Besides, the snowplows that had come to clear the streets were now just adding to the mess.

28. Are amusement park rides, such as roller coasters, becoming more dangerous?

    F A federal agency reported that the number of injuries from rides at amusement parks, fairs, and carnivals rose from 7,185 in 1985 to 10,580 in 2000. The numbers of injuries at amusement parks alone jumped from 3,720 in 1996 to 7,260 in 2000.

    G The modern roller coaster may have begun with a sled ride popular in Russia in the 1600s. The ride had two towers connected by an ice-covered track. Sleds shot down the ramp on the side of the taller tower and up the ramp on the smaller tower.

    H Attendance figures for 2001 show that of the top twenty amusement parks in the United States, eight were in Florida and seven in California. Of the other five, two each were in New Jersey and Ohio, and one was in Nevada.

    J A surprising number of amusement park injuries come from inflatable rides. These attractions, such as giant slides, get their shape when they are filled with air.

Read each paragraph. Then choose the sentence that does <u>not</u> belong in the paragraph.

29.   **1.** Have you noticed how familiar sounds have different effects during day and night? **2.** A passing siren is only annoying during the day. **3.** The siren can identify a police car, ambulance, or other emergency vehicle. **4.** At night, however, a passing siren can sound like a sad cry.

    A Sentence 1

    B Sentence 2

    C Sentence 3

    D Sentence 4

30.   **1.** Throughout the northern states, snow can be expected during at least five months. **2.** This winter, Charlie hopes to make some extra money plowing snow from driveways. **3.** He bought a snowplow for his pickup truck. **4.** He has distributed flyers all over the neighborhood to advertise his service.

    F Sentence 1

    G Sentence 2

    H Sentence 3

    J Sentence 4

Read the paragraphs and the letter and look at the numbered, underlined parts. Choose the answer that is written correctly for each underlined part.

Dolls that eat, talk, walk, and swim sound like modern developments.
(31) However, the first dolls to do these things <u>are produced</u> more than a
(32) century <u>ago. In 1824 a german inventor</u> patented a device that enabled a doll to say "mama" and "papa." In 1862 doll makers in America and other countries produced dolls that could walk. By 1880 there was a French doll
(33) that could <u>swim, another</u> could "eat." Even Thomas Edison got into the doll
(34) business with a tiny record player that <u>fit inside a doll and to make it talk</u>.

31. **A** was produced

   B were produced

   C will be produced

   D Correct as it is

32. **F** ago, in 1824. A German inventor

   G ago: in 1824 a german inventor

   H ago. In 1824 a German inventor

   J Correct as it is

33. **A** swim. another

   B swim; another

   C swim; nevertheless, another

   D Correct as it is

34. **F** fit inside a doll and made it talk

   G fit inside a doll and making it talk

   H fit inside a doll and was making it talk

   J Correct as it is

(35) My wife and I have decorated our house for <u>Halloween, our favorite holiday,</u>
(36) for several years. My parents used to say <u>that "they thought all those decorations</u>
(37) <u>were silly."</u> This year, however, is different. <u>My Dad and Mom talked theirselves</u>
(38) into putting giant spiders all over their lawn. Now we'll have to decorate <u>more creatively</u> to top their display.

35. **A** halloween, our favorite Holiday,

   B Halloween our favorite holiday

   C Halloween, our favorite holiday

   D Correct as it is

36. **F** that they thought all them decorations were silly.

   G that they thought all those decorations were silly.

   H that they "thought all them decorations were silly."

   J Correct as it is

37. **A** My Dad and Mom talked themselves

   B My dad and mom talked theirselves

   C My dad and mom talked themselves

   D Correct as it is

38. **F** most creatively

   G more creative

   H most creative

   J Correct as it is

(39) September 20 2003

Elizabeth Bennett

(40) p.o. box 1805

(41) des moines, iowa 50309

(42) Dear Ms. Bennett

(43)   Your cartoon, "A close thing," is always the first thing I

(44) read in the morning. It's the more funny thing in the

(45) whole newspaper. To my wife and I, your cartoon, more than

(46) anything else in the comic pages, will have made the rest of
the paper easier to take. I just thought I'd write and let you
know how much I like your panel. Keep up the good work!

                Sincerely yours,

                Sam Lewis

                Sam Lewis

39. **A** September, 20 2003

    B September 20, 2003

    C September 20 2003,

    D Correct as it is

40. **F** p.o. Box 1805

    G P.O. Box 1805

    H PO Box 1805

    J Correct as it is

41. **A** Des Moines Iowa 50309

    B des Moines, Iowa 50309

    C Des Moines, Iowa 50309

    D Correct as it is

42. **F** Dear Ms. Bennett:

    G Dear Ms. Bennett;

    H Dear Ms. Bennett.

    J Correct as it is

43. **A** "A Close Thing,"

    B "a Close Thing,"

    C A Close Thing,

    D Correct as it is

44. **F** more funnier

    G funnier

    H funniest

    J Correct as it is

45. **A** To my wife and myself, your

    B To my wife and I, yours

    C To my wife and me, your

    D Correct as it is

46. **F** will have made

    G makes

    H have made

    J Correct as it is

Posttest Answer Key and Evaluation Chart

This Posttest has been designed to check your mastery of the language skills studied. Circle the question numbers that you answered incorrectly and review the practice pages covering those skills.

Key

1.	A	24.	G
2.	G	25.	C
3.	C	26.	H
4.	F	27.	D
5.	B	28.	F
6.	G	29.	C
7.	A	30.	F
8.	J	31.	B
9.	C	32.	H
10.	H	33.	B
11.	D	34.	F
12.	F	35.	D
13.	B	36.	G
14.	H	37.	C
15.	D	38.	J
16.	H	39.	B
17.	A	40.	G
18.	J	41.	C
19.	D	42.	F
20.	G	43.	A
21.	A	44.	H
22.	H	45.	C
23.	D	46.	G

Tested Skills	Question Numbers	Practice Pages
pronouns	8, 45	22–25, 26–29
antecedent agreement	16	30–33
verbs	10, 31, 46	34–37, 38–41, 42–45
subject/verb agreement	6	46–49
easily confused verbs	11	50–53
adjectives and adverbs	9, 38, 44	54–57, 58–61, 62–65
use of negatives	7	66–69
sentence recognition	13	74–77, 78–81
sentence combining	18, 19, 20, 21	82–85, 86–89, 90–93
sentence clarity	34	94–97, 98–101, 102–105
topic sentences	24	110–113, 114–117
supporting sentences	26, 27, 28	118–121
sequence	22, 25	122–125
unrelated sentences	29, 30	126–129
connectives and transitions	23	130–133
proper nouns and proper adjectives	12, 32, 37	138–141, 142–145
first words and titles	43	146–149
end marks	2	154–157
commas	3, 4, 17, 35	158–161, 162–165, 166–169
semicolons and colons	33	170–173
quotations	5, 14, 36	178–181
apostrophes in contractions and possessives	1, 15	182–185, 186–189
letter parts	39, 40, 41, 42	190–193

◆ Answer Key

◆ Unit 1 Usage

◆ Lesson 1 Recognizing and Using Nouns

Page 18: 1. *Underline:* sidewalk; *Circle:* children, pictures, **2.** *Circle:* Pioneers, Great Plains, wagons, **3.** *Underline:* Miller's Department Store, sale; *Circle:* sheets, blankets, **4.** *Underline:* Candice, Big Dipper; *Circle:* stars, **5.** *Underline:* Sahara Desert; *Circle:* camels, dunes, **6.** *Underline:* Leonardo da Vinci, portrait, *Mona Lisa,* **7.** *Underline:* neighborhood, thunderstorm; *Circle:* Trees, branches, **8.** *Underline:* Andrew, Mrs. Hoffman, pride

Page 19: Answers will vary.

Page 20: 1. The Olympic Games are held every four years. **2.** How much does the Westlake Children's Zoo charge for admission? **3.** Correct, **4.** Marian Anderson served the United States as a delegate to the United Nations. **5.** President John F. Kennedy took office in 1961. **6.** Hawaii is located in the Pacific Ocean. **7.** Correct, **8–11.** Answers will vary.

Page 21: 1. B, **2.** H, **3.** A, **4.** J, **5.** A, **6.** H, **7.** C, **8.** H, **9.** B, **10.** J

◆ Lesson 2 Personal Pronouns

Page 22: 1. *Underline:* he; *Circle:* Alex, **2.** *Underline:* you; *Circle:* Phil, **3.** *Underline:* their; *Circle:* lawyers, **4.** *Underline:* her; *Circle:* Kirsten, **5.** *Underline:* they; *Circle:* citizens, **6.** *Underline:* she; *Circle:* Maria

Page 23: 1. A, **2.** A, **3.** B, **4.** B, **5.** A

Page 24: 1. *Underline:* his; *Circle:* Grandfather, **2.** *Underline:* her; *Circle:* Michelle, **3.** *Underline:* their; *Circle:* squirrels, **4.** *Underline:* their; *Circle:* students, **5.** *Underline:* its; *Circle:* mountain, **6.** my, **7.** yours, **8.** hers, **9.** your, **10.** their

Page 25: 1. B, **2.** H, **3.** A, **4.** G, **5.** D, **6.** F, **7.** D, **8.** F

◆ Lesson 3 Other Kinds of Pronouns

Page 26: 1. these, **2.** that, **3.** That, **4.** This, **5.** those, **6.** *Circle:* whom; *Arrow to:* hero, **7.** *Circle:* that; *Arrow to:* mansion, **8.** *Circle:* who; *Arrow to:* woman, **9.** *Circle:* which; *Arrow to:* country, **10.** *Circle:* which; *Arrow to:* company

Page 27: 1. *Underline:* herself; REF, **2.** *Underline:* everyone; IND, **3.** *Underline:* himself; REF, **4.** *Underline:* themselves; REF, **5.** *Underline:* Some; IND, **6.** *Underline:* most; IND, **7.** *Underline:* All; IND, **8.** *Underline:* themselves; REF

Page 28: 1. Answers may vary. Possible answers are given. **1.** these *or* those, **2.** himself, **3.** All, Some, None, *or* Most, **4.** himself, **5.** who, **6.** This *or* That, **7.** This *or* That, **8.** herself, **9.** All, Some, Most, *or* None, **10.** that, **11–15.** Answers will vary.

Page 29: 1. A, **2.** G, **3.** B, **4.** H, **5.** C, **6.** H, **7.** C, **8.** G

◆ Lesson 4 Making Pronouns Agree with Their Antecedents

Page 30: 1. *Underline:* her; *Circle:* Caitlin, **2.** *Underline:* their; *Circle:* Several, **3.** *Underline:*

they; *Circle:* fans, **4.** *Underline:* his; *Circle:* Dr. Frankenstein, **5.** *Underline:* its; *Circle:* dog, **6.** *Underline:* his, her; *Circle:* everyone, **7.** *Underline:* its; *Circle:* storm, **8.** *Underline:* their; *Circle:* Joan, Rita, **9.** *Underline:* their; *Circle:* hyena, gazelle, **10.** *Underline:* themselves; *Circle:* Most

Page 31: 1. *Underline:* she; *Circle:* model, **2.** *Underline:* who; *Circle:* millionaire, **3.** *Underline:* his or her; *Circle:* Everyone, **4.** *Underline:* their; *Circle:* Many, **5.** *Underline:* their; *Circle:* Swimmers, **6.** *Underline:* themselves; *Circle:* workers, **7.** *Underline:* their; *Circle:* Amy, Lindsey, **8.** *Underline:* his *or* her; *Circle:* Somebody, **9.** *Underline:* that; *Circle:* sweater, **10.** *Underline:* it; *Circle:* car

Page 32: 1. The teacher who took a special interest in me was Mr. Wesley. **2.** Anna Moses took up painting when she was more than 70 years old. **3.** Both Dean and Paul hardly ever answer their phones on the first ring. **4.** Correct, **5.** Most of the participants felt that their time was well spent. **6.** The music hall, which was built in 1898, is being renovated. **7.** Anybody with a password can access his or her account. **8.** When Ellen and Megan met again, they screamed and hugged. **9.** I washed this window twice because it still seemed dirty. **10.** When Terri gets up too early, she gets tired around three o'clock. **11.** Correct, **12.** Many of the audience members got to their feet and applauded.

Page 33: 1. C, **2.** J, **3.** B, **4.** F, **5.** B, **6.** G, **7.** A, **8.** H

◆ Lesson 5 Verbs

Page 34: 1. complained, repaired. **2.** is, **3.** arrive, plant, **4.** have come, are, **5.** predicted, has fallen, **6.** has been, **7.** was, got, **8.** Is, **9.** planted, **10.** fell, **11.** are, **12.** should see

Page 35: Regular: carry; move, Irregular: break; freeze; steal; drink; sing; swim; feed; teach

Page 36: 1. P, **2.** A, **3.** P, **4.** P, **5.** A, **6.** P, **7–9:** Sentences will vary, but the listed verbs must be used.

Page 37: 1. D, **2.** G, **3.** B, **4.** H, **5.** A, **6.** H, **7.** D, **8.** J

◆ Lesson 6 Verbs and Their Tenses

Page 38: 1. hide, **2.** asked, **3.** has, **4.** will pick, **5.** know, **6.** expected, **7.** will notify

Page 39: 1. C, **2.** F, **3.** D, **4.** G, **5.** C, **6.** J

Page 40: 1. was sleeping, **2.** answered, **3.** am working, **4.** will be practicing, **5.** was trying, **6.** failed, **7.** go, **8.** were buying, **9.** pressed, **10.** was apologizing

Page 41: 1. B, **2.** G, **3.** A, **4.** H, **5.** D, **6.** J, **7.** A, **8.** H

◆ Lesson 7 Perfect Tenses of Verbs

Page 42: 1. *Underline:* had dressed, heard; *Write:* had dressed, **2.** *Underline:* look, will have worked, gives; *Write:* will have worked, **3.** *Underline:* has studied; *Write:* has studied,

4. *Underline:* have sent, may get; *Write:* have sent, **5.** *Underline:* was opened, had met; *Write:* had met, **6.** *Underline:* will appear, will have played; *Write:* will have played

Page 43: 1. has worked, **2.** has rung, **3.** had experienced, **4.** predicted, **5.** will have considered, **6.** will leave, **7.** has painted, **8.** had built, **9.** bowled, **10.** have found, **11.** had read, **12.** has enjoyed, **13.** will have traveled, **14.** have lived, **15.** had lived, **16.** will have finished, **17.** had developed, **18.** had gone

Page 44: 1. B, **2.** A, **3.** A, **4.** B, **5.** had built, **6.** will have planned, **7.** had used, **8.** had blown, **9.** had beaten, **10.** have grown

Page 45: 1. B, **2.** F, **3.** C, **4.** H, **5.** C, **6.** J, **7.** B, **8.** G

◆ **Lesson 8 Agreement of Subjects and Verbs**

Page 46: 1. *Circle:* sun; *Underline:* rises, S, **2.** *Circle:* vines; *Underline:* climb, P, **3.** *Circle:* Scientists; *Underline:* search, P, **4.** *Circle:* mob; *Underline:* gathers, S, **5.** *Circle:* questions; *Underline:* are, P, **6.** *Circle:* walkway; *Underline:* leads, S, **7.** *Circle:* you; *Underline:* let, S, **8.** *Circle:* kitchens; *Underline:* were, P, **9.** *Circle:* I; *Underline:* write, P

Page 47: 1. *Circle:* row; *Underline:* stands, **2.** *Circle:* shouts; *Underline:* were, **3.** *Circle:* movie; *Underline:* Does, **4.** *Circle:* Tickets; *Underline:* have, **5.** *Circle:* Jamal; *Underline:* thinks, **6.** *Circle:* calls; *Underline:* were, **7.** *Circle:* Clues; *Underline:* have, **8.** *Circle:* girl; *Underline:* Does, **9.** *Circle:* members; *Underline:* agree,

10. *Circle:* Everyone; *Underline:* likes, **11.** *Circle:* students; *Underline:* are, **12.** *Circle:* dogs; *Underline:* play, **13.** *Circle:* strings; *Underline:* were, **14.** *Circle:* children; *Underline:* have

Page 48: 1. *Circle:* crackers, bread; *Underline:* is, **2.** *Circle:* gloves, sweater; *Underline:* were, **3.** *Circle:* cake, cookies; *Underline:* appeal, **4.** *Circle:* children, father; *Underline:* knows, **5.** *Circle:* ghost, monsters; *Underline:* are, **6.** cope, **7.** fills, **8.** lie, **9.** follows, **10.** run, **11.** brighten, **12.** represents

Page 49: 1. C, **2.** H, **3.** B, **4.** F, **5.** C, **6.** F, **7.** D, **8.** G

◆ **Lesson 9 Easily Confused Verbs**

Page 50: 1. sit, **2.** accepted, **3.** risen, **4.** sat, **5.** set, **6.** raised, **7.** accept, **8.** rose, **9.** set

Page 51: 1. B, **2.** A, **3.** B, **4.** A, **5.** B, **6.** B, **7.** Set, **8.** rises, **9.** set, **10.** accept, **11.** have, **12.** sat

Page 52: 1. The seller accepted the offer, so the house is ours! **2.** I would have helped you, if I had known you were in trouble. **3.** The movers set the boxes on the dining room floor. **4.** The grocery store has raised the prices on their name brand items. **5.** Correct, **6.** Correct, **7.** You should not have been playing catch inside the house. **8.** Driving was made dangerous by the dense fog that had risen. **9.** All the kittens except the small calico have been adopted. **10.** The old mansion sits on a hill overlooking the valley. **11.** Correct, **12.** Our team would have won if we had kicked a field goal.

Page 53: 1. B, **2.** H, **3.** A, **4.** J, **5.** C, **6.** G, **7.** D, **8.** G

◆ Lesson 10 Adjectives

Page 54: 1. new, larger, old, **2.** Every, yellow, entire, **3.** three, cozy, several, round, **4.** weather, heavy, high, **5.** more intelligent, **6.** fierce, blue, **7.** four, oak, wooden, **8.** Frugal, least expensive, **9.** happier, **10.** ripest, juiciest

Page 55: 1. lovelier, **2.** dullest, **3.** most bashful, **4.** worst, **5.** more beautiful, **6.** closest, **7.** flatter, **8.** bluer, **9.** Correct, **10.** better, **11.** more, **12.** smaller

Page 56: 1. fastest, **2.** rustier, **3.** fresh, **4.** largest, **5.** cheaper, **6.** more desirable, **7.** more powerful, **8.** dressiest, **9.** healthier, **10.** longest, **11.** Great, **12.** most expensive, **13.** better, **14.** prettiest, **15.** hairy, Paragraph descriptions will vary.

Page 57: 1. B, **2.** J, **3.** C, **4.** H, **5.** D, **6.** F, **7.** D, **8.** H

◆ Lesson 11 Adverbs

Page 58: 1. lazily, **2.** scarcely, **3.** recently, **4.** more often, **5.** completely, **6.** daily, **7.** most deeply, **8.** expectantly, **9.** unusually, **10.** not

Page 59: Adverbs: never, daily, scarcely, **Comparative forms:** more evenly, better, later, **Superlative forms:** least, most bravely, most efficiently, **10.** *Underline:* quickly; Correct, **11.** *Underline:* more better; better, **12.** *Underline:* most farthest; farthest, **13.** *Underline:* partially; Correct, **14.** *Underline:* most badly; badly,

15. *Underline:* earliest; early, **16.** *Underline:* most best; best

Page 60: Answers will vary. Possible answers are given. **1.** clearly, **2.** quickly, **3.** thoroughly, **4.** fast, **5.** now, **6.** frighteningly, **7.** quite, **8.** surprisingly, **9.** undeniably, **10.** almost, **11.** now, **12.** softly, **13.** better, **14.** ever, **15.** tomorrow, **16.** most often, **17.** barely, **18.** wildly, **19.** more loudly, **20.** most frequently

Page 61: 1. C, **2.** F, **3.** B, **4.** J, **5.** C, **6.** J, **7.** A, **8.** H

◆ Lesson 12 Adjective or Adverb?

Page 62: 1. *Circle:* every, *Write:* ADV, **2.** *Circle:* slipped, *Write:* ADV, **3.** *Circle:* fellow, *Write:* ADJ, **4.** *Circle:* started, *Write:* ADV, **5.** *Circle:* pace, *Write:* ADJ, **6.** *Circle:* hands, *Write:* ADJ, **7.** *Circle:* responded, *Write:* ADV, **8.** *Circle:* prepared, *Write:* ADV, **9.** *Circle:* shift, *Write:* ADJ, **10.** *Circle:* person, *Write:* ADJ, **11.** *Circle:* lapped, *Write:* ADV

Page 63: 1. most generously, **2.** darkest, **3.** more peaceful, **4.** wisely, **5.** more firmly, **6.** good, **7.** easier, **8.** abruptly, **9.** more fluently, **10.** fairly, **11.** well, **12.** more fearful, **13.** most loyal

Page 64: 1. patiently, **2.** more patient, **3.** most patient, **4.** most highly, **5.** highest, **6.** highly, **7.** quiet, **8.** more quiet, **9.** quietly, **10.** sooner, **11.** loudly, **12.** kindest, **13.** earlier, **14.** softly, **15.** bravely, **16.** carefully, **17.** better, **18.** most excellent

Page 65: 1. D, **2.** F, **3.** B, **4.** H, **5.** C, **6.** J, **7.** A, **8.** G

◆ Lesson 13 Using Negative Words Correctly

Page 66: 1. *Circle:* scarcely, nobody, **2.** *Circle:* can't, never, **3.** C, **4.** C, **5.** *Circle:* never, nothing, **6.** *Circle:* isn't, no, **7.** *Circle:* couldn't, nowhere, **8.** *Circle:* didn't, no, **9.** *Circle:* doesn't, nothing, **10.** C

Page 67: 1. any, **2.** ever, **3.** anywhere, **4.** any, **5.** anybody, **6.** anyone, **7.** could, **8.** were, **9.** anything, **10.** any, **11.** A, **12.** A, **13.** B, **14.** B, **15.** A

Page 68: Corrections will vary. Possible answers are provided. **1.** Correct, **2.** Alicia couldn't find anywhere to hang the huge poster. *or* Alicia could find nowhere to hang the huge poster. **3.** This project can't, in any way, be considered a failure. *or* This project can in no way be considered a failure. **4.** Correct, **5.** I never asked for anything for dessert. *or* I asked for nothing for dessert. **6.** Correct, **7.** Laura won't ever fit into that jacket again. Laura will never fit into that jacket again. **8.** The principal can't make any exceptions to the school rules. The principal can make no exceptions to the school rules. **9.** Fresh strawberries aren't available in any of the grocery stores today. Fresh strawberries are available in none of the grocery stores today.

Page 69: 1. B, **2.** G, **3.** A, **4.** J, **5.** A, **6.** H, **7.** C, **8.** J

◆ Unit 1 Assessment

Pages 71–73: 1. B, **2.** F, **3.** D, **4.** G, **5.** C, **6.** F, **7.** C, **8.** J, **9.** C, **10.** G, **11.** B, **12.** F, **13.** D, **14.** H, **15.** A, **16.** J, **17.** C, **18.** G, **19.** A, **20.** H, **21.** B, **22.** H, **23.** A, **24.** G, **25.** C, **26.** J

◆ Unit 2 Sentence Formation

◆ Lesson 1 Complete Sentences and Fragments

Page 74: 1. CS (*Underline:* Mrs. Munson; *Circle:* owns the laundromat on Fourth Street), **2.** F, **3.** F, **4.** CS (*Underline:* My brother; *Circle:* is moving to Alaska), **5.** F, **6.** CS (*Underline:* The new movie theater; *Circle:* opened last Friday), **7.** F, **8.** F, **9.** F

Page 75: Answers will vary for numbers 1, 3, and 4. Possible answers are given. **1.** The laundromat is next to DiNardo's Pizza Parlor. **2.** Correct, **3.** Maria is going to brunch with her family because her mother invited her. **4.** Carrie wanted to see the elephants before the circus left town. **5.** Correct

Page 76: 1. Add a predicate. **2.** I'll start chopping the peppers after you make the rice. **3.** We stopped by the hardware store to see our cousin. **4.** Add a subject. **5.** Jacques realized that he'd left his keys inside as he was shutting the door. **6.** Add a predicate. **7.** Combine the fragment with a complete sentence. **8.** Add a subject. **9.** Old Bill the pirate gets sentimental when he smells the ocean. **10.** I got lost outside of Chicago because I didn't have a map. **11.** Add a subject and a helping verb. **12.** Add a subject and a helping verb.

Page 77: 1. C, **2.** J, **3.** C, **4.** F, **5.** A, **6.** G

◆ Lesson 2 Run-On Sentences

Page 78: 1. *Underline:* The train is late, **2.** *Underline:* I don't know French, **3.** *Underline:* The Regal Cinema closed down, **4.** *Underline:*

Paula is leaving for Brazil on Tuesday,
5. *Underline:* Morrice is very athletic
6. *Underline:* Ian went to Boston, **7.** *Underline:*
Ms. Glover was my supervisor, **8.** *Underline:*
They don't have chocolate, **9.** RO, **10.** CS,
11. CS, **12.** RO, **13.** RO

Page 79: Answers will vary. Possible answers
are given. **1.** Frieda got a flashy new car; I saw
it yesterday. **2.** The yellow dress is on sale;
however, it doesn't fit quite right. **3.** The train
conductor punched my ticket, and he put it
above my seat. **4.** Bryan paid with a twenty,
but the cashier forgot to give back his change.
5. Mary ordered lasagna, and Joy asked for
spaghetti with meatballs. **6.** Be careful on
Preston Road. It's still under construction.
7. Knock on the door; the buzzer is broken.

Page 80: 1. A, **2.** B, **3.** A, **4.** B, **5.** B

The corrected paragraph may vary slightly
from the following:

The coffee house was filled with interesting
people. A young couple sat by the window;
they looked like they were arguing. A worried
student had her books spread out in one of
the booths. She was reading and writing
notes. An older man sat at a small table in the
back. He kept looking up. Was he waiting for
someone?

Page 81: 1. B, **2.** J, **3.** C, **4.** G, **5.** C, **6.** J

◆ Lesson 3 Sentence Combining: Compound Sentence Parts

Page 82: 1. *Underline:* volunteers at the
homeless shelter, *Write:* Ryan and Lisa

volunteer at the homeless shelter. **2.** *Underline:*
Heather, *Write:* Heather overslept and was
late for work. **3.** *Underline:* comes with every
dinner, *Write:* A salad and a vegetable come
with every dinner. **4.** *Underline:* made driving
dangerous, *Write:* The icy roads and drifting
snow made driving dangerous.

Page 83: 1. *Underline:* The trip into the
wilderness was; B, **2.** *Underline:* Justin bought,
for his girlfriend; A, **3.** *Underline:* The couple
invited many, to their wedding; B, **4.** A,
5. *Underline:* The music shop, instruments; A,
6. *Underline:* Our store promises; B

Page 84: 1. I need to buy more film and an
extra battery for my camera. **2.** I asked for
iced tea, but the waitress gave me coffee.
3. Mr. Franklin collects rare and unusual
coins. **4.** The magician performed many
fantastic tricks and amazed the audience.
5. Add the chopped nuts and the chocolate
chips to the cookie dough. **6.** Correct,
7. The sports league presents awards every
year at a huge, well-attended picnic.

Page 85: 1. A, **2.** H, **3.** C, **4.** J

◆ Lesson 4 Sentence Combining: Subordinate Clauses

Page 86: 1. DC, **2.** DC, **3.** DC, **4.** IC, **5.** DC, **6.** DC,
7. IC, **8.** DC, **9.** DC, **10.** DC, **11.** IC, **12.** DC

Page 87: 1. A, **2.** B, **3.** B, **4.** A

Page 88: Revised sentences may vary. Possible
answers are provided. **1.** Hernando enjoyed
fishing in the cove because it was quiet and
peaceful there. **2.** Correct, **3.** After my truck
ran out of gas, I had to walk four miles to the

nearest town. **4.** Since Raymond neglected to level the ground properly, the patio stones are uneven. **5.** We must leave right now, or I will be late. *or* Unless we leave right now, I will be late. **6.** Correct

Page 89: 1. C, **2.** G, **3.** D, **4.** J

♦ Lesson 5   Sentence Combining: Adding Modifiers

Page 90: 1. *Underline:* cabin; We always rent a cabin near the Smoky Mountains for the summer. **2.** *Underline:* entry; One ornate entry in the art exhibit stood out from the rest. **3.** *Underline:* basket; My cat keeps her kittens in a basket under the porch. **4.** *Underline:* seats; During the play-offs, only a few seats in the upper deck were empty. **5.** *Underline:* spring; The water in the underground spring is cool and refreshing.

Page 91: 1. C, **2.** A, **3.** E, **4.** B, **5.** D, Placement of adverbs and adverb phrases may vary for items 6 and 7. **6.** Two linemen lunged frantically at the loose football. **7.** Our cruise ship stopped in San Juan for three days.

Page 92: Placement of adverbs and adverb phrases may vary. **1.** Sophia slowly and carefully reconstructed the broken vase. **2.** The magician appeared to walk through a stone wall. **3.** Correct, **4.** As a consultant, Mr. Getz traveled extensively all over the world. **5.** Correct, **6.** We stopped for coffee after the movie. **7.** The skier smoothly and gracefully sped down the steep slope.

Page 93: 1. B, **2.** F, **3.** D, **4.** H

♦ Lesson 6   Sentence Clarity: Misplaced Modifiers

Page 94: 1. Any customer with a good credit rating can order a dining room set. **2.** I saw a brown squirrel hiding acorns under a bush. **3.** Several coins that fell from Zubin's pocket rolled into the street. **4.** The pencils in that box are sharp, but they have no erasers. **5.** The story is about a pirate marooned on a desert island. **6.** Always barking, our neighbors' dog irritates us.

Page 95: 1. B, **2.** A, **3.** B, **4.** A, **5.** B, **6.** B, **7.** B, **8.** A

Page 96: 1. B, **2.** H, **3.** A, **4 and 5.** Answers will vary. Possible answers are given. **4.** Cutting the lawn, Allen saw a skunk cross the lawn in front of him. **5.** Lying in her pocket, Ilona's cell phone rang during an orchestra concert.

Page 97: 1. C, **2.** F, **3.** B, **4.** J, **5.** B, **6.** H

♦ Lesson 7   Sentence Clarity: Parallel Structure

Page 98: 1. A, **2.** B, **3.** A, **4.** B, **5.** B, **6.** A

Page 99: 1. B, **2.** J, **3.** A, **4.** F, **5.** A, **6.** G

Page 100: 1. B, **2.** G, **3.** C, **4.** J, **5.** B, **6.** G, **7.** A, **8.** H

Page 101: 1. A, **2.** J, **3.** A, **4.** H, **5.** C, **6.** F

♦ Lesson 8   Sentence Clarity: Verbosity and Repetition

Page 102: 1. B, **2.** A, **3.** B, **4.** B, **5.** A

◆ Answer Key *continued*

Page 103: 1. B, **2.** H, **3.** A, **4.** G, **5.** B, **6.** F

Page 104: 1. B, **2.** J, **3.** C, **4.** F, **5–7.** Answers will vary. Possible answers are given. **5.** Most of these problems could be avoided with correctly placed traffic signs. **6.** The guest comedian on the late-night show delivered a boring monologue with repetitive jokes. **7.** Carmakers bring out new vehicles every year to tempt car owners to move up to the latest models.

Page 105: 1. C, **2.** G, **3.** A, **4.** J

◆ Unit 2 Assessment

Pages 107–109: 1. C, **2.** J, **3.** A, **4.** G, **5.** C, **6.** G, **7.** B, **8.** H, **9.** C, **10.** F, **11.** C, **12.** F, **13.** B, **14.** F, **15.** C, **16.** J

◆ Unit 3 Paragraph Development

◆ Lesson 1 The Main Idea of a Paragraph

Page 110: 1. *Underline:* Gloria really knows how to travel light; C, **2.** *Underline:* The Spamarama, held each May in Austin, Texas, is an occasion for many unusual contests; G

Page 111: 1. D, **2.** E, **3.** C, **4.** A, **5.** B

Page 112: Answers will vary. Possible answers are given. **1.** Amy and Lisa have been in competition for years. **2.** Gail had a terrible night last night. **3.** Matt is addicted to sugar. **4.** We can learn many lessons from children's stories. **5.** Plants are good for us in many ways.

Page 113: 1. B, **2.** J, **3.** D

◆ Lesson 2 Finding the Topic Sentence

Page 114: 1. Surely, Frida Kahlo and Diego Rivera are one of the most interesting couples in Mexican history. **2.** Falling in love and catching the flu have a lot in common.

Page 115: 1. D, **2.** H

Page 116: Answers will vary. Possible answers are given. **1.** Be careful when you use a table saw or a band saw. **2.** The effects of the prolonged drought were obvious. **3.** Karen and Jonas are as different as friends can be. **4.** Our stay at the cheap hotel was a nightmare.

Page 117: 1. A, **2.** H, **3.** C

◆ Lesson 3 Supporting Sentences

Page 118: 1. Reasons

Page 119: 1. sensory details, C

Page 120: Answers will vary.

Page 121: 1. B, **2.** J, **3.** C

◆ Lesson 4 Recognizing Sequence

Page 122: The wording of answers may vary. **1.** The soccer team won the game that put them in the national championships. **2.** The coach showed up and revived everyone's spirits.

Page 123: 1. C, D, A, B, **2.** F, H, G, J

Page 124: 1. 2, 1, 4, 3, **2.** 3, 4, 1, 2, **3.** 1, 4, 2, 3,

4. 4, 3, 2, 1

Page 125: 1. B, **2.** J, **3.** D

◆ Lesson 5 Identifying an Unrelated Sentence

Page 126: Wording of answers will vary. Possible answers are given. **1.** There were three kinds of engines in early cars. **2.** Electric batteries were clean, quiet, and easy to start, but slow. *or* Steam engines were clean and fast, but their range was limited to about 150 miles. *or* Gasoline engines were fast and easy to start, and their range was unlimited, but they broke down regularly and were dirty. **3.** Trains also used steam engines.

Page 127: 1. B, **2.** B, **3.** B, **4.** A

Page 128: 1. *Cross out:* The resort makes snow on days when natural snow is scarce. **2.** Correct, **3.** *Cross out:* Sugar cane is one of Hawaii's most important crops. **4.** *Cross out:* One of his best-known plays, *You Can't Take It with You*, was recently put on by the Westview Little Theater.

Page 129: 1. D, **2.** H, **3.** A

◆ Lesson 6 Transition Words and Phrases

Page 130: 1. Therefore; C, **2.** however; F

Page 131: 1. E, **2.** B, **3.** A, **4.** C, **5.** D

Page 132: 1. B, **2.** J, **3.** A, **4.** J, **5.** B

Page 133: 1. C, **2.** G, **3.** A

◆ Unit 3 Assessment

Pages 135–137: 1. C, **2.** J, **3.** B, **4.** G, **5.** C, **6.** F, **7.** C, **8.** F, **9.** D

◆ Unit 4 Capitalization

◆ Lesson 1 Capitalizing Proper Nouns and *I*

Page 138: 1. uncle austin, dr. klein, **2.** i, aunt jackie, **3.** j. r. quinn, **4.** princess diana, **5.** mr. tony asaro, **6.** ms. lynne martin, **7.** sir arthur conan doyle, sherlock holmes, **8.** cousin amy

Page 139: 1. Correct, **2.** President Richard M. Nixon, **3.** Julia D. Grant, **4.** Aunt Peggy, **5.** Dr. William Stewart, **6.** Justice Ruth Bader Ginsberg, **7.** Correct, **8.** Johann Sebastian Bach, **9.** James A. Brennan, **10.** Cousin Luke, **11.** Ms. Erica Kane, **12.** B, **13.** H, **14.** B

Page 140: 1. We rented the apartment from Mr. Kevin Hayes. **2.** Will Kwame and Isaac be working on the project with us? **3.** This is an excellent biography of General John J. Pershing. **4.** Does Cindy Wiles ever arrive on time? **5.** My sister and I were always getting into trouble with our neighbor, Mr. Rufus. **6.** Tell Private Cox to report to Sergeant Riley. **7.** B, **8.** H, **9.** B, **10.** J

Page 141: 1. C, **2.** J, **3.** B, **4.** F, **5.** B, **6.** F, **7.** B, **8.** H

◆ Lesson 2 Capitalizing Proper Nouns and Proper Adjectives

Page 142: 1. Groundhog Day, **2.** Pittsburgh, Pennsylvania, **3.** Clayton Building, **4.** Lake

Huron, **5.** French bread, **6.** Tower Bridge, **7.** eastern Missouri, **8.** Correct

Page 143: 1. B, **2.** H, **3.** A, **4.** united states census bureau, **5.** tuesday, newton chamber, commerce, **6.** special olympics, fulton center, **7.** moore trucking company, **8.** zephyr appliance company, sidney street

Page 144: 1. The bus crossed the Mackinac Bridge and headed into northern Michigan. **2.** My brother graduated from Hudson High School last June. **3.** The countries of Brazil and Argentina are in South America. **4.** Members of the United Auto Workers marched in the parade on Labor Day. **5.** Joshua spent two years as a volunteer for the Peace Corps in Nicaragua. **6.** We stayed at the Mountain View Inn near Pikes Peak last summer. **7.** My mother raises African violets. **8.** The Imperial Carpet Cleaning Company did an excellent job on our Oriental rug. **9.** The Kentucky Derby is run on the first Saturday in May. **10.** The climate in the Southwest is drier than that of the Northwest. **11.** Some pictures on the walls of European caves were painted during the Stone Age. **12.** The Curran Theatre is on Geary Street in the city of San Francisco.

Page 145: 1. B, **2.** F, **3.** C, **4.** J, **5.** B, **6.** H, **7.** D, **8.** F

◆ Lesson 3 Capitalizing First Words, Titles, and Abbreviations

Page 146: 1. B, **2.** A, **3.** A, **4.** B, **5.** A, **6.** B

Page 147: 1. "With or Without You", **2.** *The*

Fellowship of the Ring, **3.** "Not in Vain", **4.** Correct, **5.** "Home Improvement", **6.** "Hearts and Hands", **7.** Correct, **8.** *A Chorus Line,* **9.** *Shadows on the Rock,* **10.** B, **11.** H, **12.** A, **13.** J

Page 148: 1. "My mailing address is P.O. Box 152," said Mrs. Magee. **2.** *The West Wing* is Julia's favorite television program. **3.** Our neighbors bought tickets to see the stage production of *The Lion King.* **4.** She asked, "Where is this month's issue of *National Geographic*?" **5.** "The show will begin promptly at 8:30 P.M.," said the announcer. **6.** My daughter memorized the poem, "Paul Revere's Ride." **7.** "*To Kill a Mockingbird* is a powerful book," replied the librarian. **8.** The toddler whined, "Grandma, I want more cookies." **9.** At the end of the program, the choir sang Beethoven's "Ode to Joy." **10.** We always read our local newspaper, *The Sun Journal.* **11.** "The Pit and the Pendulum" is one of Poe's scariest short stories. **12.** Send the subscription for *Archeology Today* to P.O. Box 515.

Page 149: 1. B, **2.** F, **3.** D, **4.** H, **5.** C, **6.** G

◆ Unit 4 Assessment

Pages 151–153: 1. C, **2.** F, **3.** D, **4.** H, **5.** B, **6.** F, **7.** B, **8.** H, **9.** B, **10.** J, **11.** C, **12.** G, **13.** B, **14.** J, **15.** A, **16.** J, **17.** C, **18.** G, **19.** B, **20.** F

◆ Unit 5 Punctuation

◆ Lesson 1 End Marks

Page 154: 1. ? **2.** ! **3.** . **4.** ! **5.** ? **6.** . **7.** ! **8.** . **9.** ! **10.** .

Page 155: 1. A, **2.** F, **3.** C, **4.** G, **5.** D, **6.** G, **7.** A, **8.** B, **9.** A, **10.** A, **11.** B, **12.** B

Page 156: Sentences will vary. They should relate to the given situations and end with the proper end marks.

Page 157: 1. C, **2.** G, **3.** C, **4.** F, **5.** A, **6.** H, **7.** B, **8.** G, **9.** D, **10.** H

◆ Lesson 2 Commas: Compound Sentences and Introductory Words

Page 158: 1. Correct, **2.** We wanted to see the movie, but all the tickets were sold. **3.** I foolishly left my umbrella at the office, and it rained all evening. **4.** Samia often visits the outdoor market, for it reminds her of her homeland. **5.** Correct, **6.** Do you file your tax return early, or do you wait for the deadline? **7.** Joe is certified as a mechanic, but he also does auto body work. **8.** Correct

Page 159: 1. To raise money for his favorite charity, Christopher organized a 10K race. **2.** For one thing, swampland is no place to build a beach house. **3.** Yes, I do have change for a dollar. **4.** Swinging wildly, Francis whacked the baseball out of the park. **5.** After the frost my delicate plants looked rather wilted. **6.** For that matter, you've been working overtime all week. **7.** B, **8.** A, **9.** A, **10.** A

Page 160: 1–4. Answers will vary, but each must include a comma at the end of the given independent clause, before the connecting word. **5.** C, **6.** Insert commas after *No* and *anymore*. **7.** Place *X* on comma. **8.** Place *X* on comma; insert comma after *tired*.

Page 161: 1. C, **2.** F, **3.** D, **4.** G, **5.** D, **6.** H, **7.** B, **8.** J

◆ Lesson 3 Commas: Series and Parenthetical Expressions

Page 162: 1. A, **2.** A, **3.** B, **4.** B, **5.** A

Page 163: 1. He decided, however, not to join us for dinner. **2.** Oh, did I say something I shouldn't have? **3.** The citrus grove, as the picture indicates, lies just beyond the house. **4.** Indeed, that is the price for this nearly new truck. **5.** Molly has a reason, I suppose, for skipping the organizational meeting. **6.** Politicians, generally speaking, should consider their constituents. **7.** Whatever his weaknesses are, Lloyd is an excellent auditor. **8.** The fall foliage will be very colorful, although very briefly, in this area. **9.** I'll choose a repair shop more carefully next time, to be sure. **10.** In conclusion, we thank you for participating in our survey today. **11.** Do intelligent people, she wondered, act that way? **12.** Well, maybe just a bit of chocolate cake won't add too many calories. **13.** We could, of course, fly directly to Los Angeles and skip the layovers. **14.** He would have come, Arthur explained, if he hadn't missed the bus.

Page 164: 1. B, **2.** J, **3.** C, **4.** H, **5.** Newspapers, magazines, and paperbacks filled the entire bookcase. **6.** The price, I guess, is more than I can afford to pay. **7.** Correct, **8.** Dozens of unhappy, dissatisfied, impatient customers waited in the complaint line. **9.** Do you know, for instance, the capitals of Oregon, Montana, or Missouri? **10.** The bicycle hit a bump, wobbled slightly, and slipped sideways.

Page 165: 1. C, **2.** F, **3.** B, **4.** G, **5.** B, **6.** H, **7.** A, **8.** F

◆ Lesson 4 Other Uses of Commas

Page 166: 1. Insert commas after *Avenue, Bob,* **2.** Insert commas after *me, Felice, Diego,* **3.** Insert comma after *desk,* **4.** Insert commas after *Albuquerque, Mexico,* **5.** B, **6.** A, **7.** A, **8.** B

Page 167: 1. *Underline:* a sea food restaurant; *Write:* The Crab Shack, **2.** *Underline:* my neighbors; *Write:* Bill and Helene, **3.** *Underline:* a man of few words; *Write:* Deborah's father, **4.** *Underline:* the Whales; *Write:* his favorite team, **5.** *Underline:* or a special corn bread; *Write:* hoecake, **6.** Insert commas after Tony, barber, **7.** Insert commas after *restaurant, Garden,* **8.** Insert commas after *custodians, Olivera,* **9.** Insert commas after *club, Wheels,* **10.** Insert commas after *home, colonial,* **11.** Insert commas after *fry, fish,* **12.** Insert commas after *Columbus, Ohio*

Page 168: 1. The PTA president, Ali Takla, has requested more parental involvement. **2.** Owen's job, assistant zoo keeper, reflected his deep love of animals. **3.** Natasha took her car to the closest repair shop, Al's Tire and Battery. **4.** Ron's prized possession, a battered guitar, leaned against his chair. **5.** One of my favorite bushes is the ilex, or holly. **6–11:** Answers will vary. Commas must set off all underlined words and any appositives.

Page 169: 1. B, **2.** F, **3.** C, **4.** H, **5.** A, **6.** H

◆ Lesson 5 Semicolons and Colons

Page 170: 1. Insert semicolon after *hard,* **2.** Insert semicolons after *T-shirts, caps,* **3.** Insert semicolon after *morning,* **4.** Insert semicolon after *speaker,* **5.** Insert semicolons after *Lange, Black,* **6.** Insert semicolon after *edible,* **7.** Insert semicolon after *o'clock,* **8.** Insert semicolons after *sister, brother,* **9.** Insert semicolon after *meeting*

Page 171: 1. Place *X* over colon, **2.** Insert colon in *8:14,* **3.** Insert colon after *following,* **4.** Insert semicolon after *use,* **5.** Insert semicolon after *out,* **6.** B, **7.** A, **8.** A, **9.** A

Page 172: The following students should report to the office: Jo Andrews, Pat Ryan, and Joe Lopez. **2.** The book was good; the movie was better. **3.** Frank waited in the car with the engine running; finally, he turned it off. **4.** You will find newspapers, magazines, and yearbooks in the reading room; novels, biographies, and mysteries in the main room; and picture books in the children's room. **5.** Although the play started late, it ended exactly at 10:00 P.M. **6.** Waves were high, and the small boat was taking in water. **7.** Correct, **8.** Karen makes fancy meals; for example, she cooked Beef Wellington last night. **9.** Greg has an interview at Kenner Industries, a company near the freeway. **10.** On our vacation we went to New York, New York; Portland, Maine; and Hartford, Connecticut.

Page 173: 1. D, **2.** G, **3.** A, **4.** F, **5.** A, **6.** H

◆ Unit 5 Assessment

Page 175–177: 1. B, **2.** G, **3.** C, **4.** G, **5.** A, **6.** H, **7.** C, **8.** J, **9.** B, **10.** J, **11.** A, **12.** J, **13.** C, **14.** F, **15.** D, **16.** G, **17.** A, **18.** H, **19.** D, **20.** J, **21.** A, **22.** H, **23.** A

◆ Unit 6 Writing Conventions

◆ Lesson 1 Writing Quotations

Page 178: 1. D; The bank teller said, "Please endorse your check." **2.** D; "What an amazing deal that was!" exclaimed Liz. **3.** I, **4.** D; Tyler asked, "Which department handles customer complaints?" **5.** I, **6.** D; "How often do you check your e-mail?" asked Kendra. **7.** D; The astronomer announced, "There has been an important discovery!" **8.** I, **9.** D; "This beach is always busy on summer weekends," said Hasan. **10.** I, **11.** D; Allie called to her friend, "Hurry or you'll miss the bus!" **12.** D; "This VCR hasn't worked well since I bought it," the customer complained.

Page 179: 1. said, **2.** ring, **3.** great, James, **4.** shouted, **5.** B, **6.** B, **7.** A, **8.** A

Page 180: 1. Adam said, "Let's paint this room green." **2.** Correct, **3.** "Is green a neutral color?" asked Roz. **4.** "It may not be neutral," said Adam, "but I'm tired of white walls." **5.** Roz admitted, "I think I'm ready for a change." **6.** "I just love the room's new look!" exclaimed Roz. **7.** Correct, **8–10.** Sentences will vary. Be sure that all punctuation and capitalization rules are followed and that sentences match the directions.

Page 181: 1. B, **2.** F, **3.** A, **4.** J, **5.** D, **6.** H, **7.** C, **8.** G

◆ Lesson 2 Using the Apostrophe: Writing Contractions

Page 182: 1. *Underline:* hasn't; *Write:* has + not, **2.** *Underline:* It's; *Write:* It + is, **3.** *Underline:* shouldn't; *Write:* should + not, **4.** *Underline:* isn't; *Write:* is + not, **5.** *Underline:* couldn't; *Write:* could + not

Page 183: 1. B, **2.** A, **3.** B, **4.** A, **5.** A, **6.** B, **7.** its, **8.** they're, **9.** It's, **10.** their, **11.** they're, **12.** it's, **13.** they're, **14.** there, **15.** it's, **16.** its

Page 184: 1. *Underline:* was not; *Write:* wasn't, **2.** *Underline:* it is; *Write:* it's, **3.** *Underline:* will not; *Write:* won't, **4.** *Underline:* were not; *Write:* weren't, **5.** *Underline:* we will; *Write:* we'll, **6.** *Underline:* you are; *Write:* you're, **7.** *Circle:* wer'e; *Write:* we're, **8.** *Circle:* Weve'; *Write:* We've, **9.** *Circle:* youl'l; *Write:* you'll, **10.** *Circle:* ca'nt; *Write:* can't, **11.** *Circle:* yo'uve; *Write:* you've, **12.** *Circle:* shes'; *Write:* she's, **13.** *Circle:* Its; *Write:* It's, **14.** *Circle:* the'ir; *Write:* they're

Page 185: 1. D, **2.** F, **3.** B, **4.** H, **5.** D, **6.** J, **7.** C, **8.** G

◆ Lesson 3 Using the Apostrophe: Writing Possessive Nouns

Page 186: 1. the workers' tools, **2.** the senator's aides, **3.** the graduates' diplomas, **4.** Myra's smile, **5.** the bear's cave, **6.** the geese's flight path, **7.** the students' tests, **8.** the hunters' decoys, **9.** the men's tennis match

Page 187: 1. A, **2.** B, **3.** B, **4.** A, **5.** A,
6. *Underline:* Gordons; *Write:* Gordons',
7. *Underline:* speakers'; *Write:* speaker's,
8. *Underline:* Christies; *Write:* Christie's,
9. *Underline:* actor's; *Write:* actors',
10. *Underline:* musician's'; *Write:* musicians'

Page 188: 1. Rich's dog is gentle, but its bark can sound vicious. **2.** Correct, **3.** It is the Browns' contention that the fault cannot be theirs. **4.** Correct, **5.** The congressman's Web site posts his stand on the issues.
6-10. Sentences will vary. **6.** *Underline:* opinions of the voters, *Use in sentence:* voters' opinions, **7.** *Underline:* toys that belong to the children, *Use in sentence:* childrens' toys, **8.** *Underline:* budget of the organization, *Use in sentence:* organization's budget, **9.** *Underline:* home of the skunks, *Use in sentence:* skunks' home, **10.** *Underline:* energy that belonged to the runners, *Use in sentence:* runners' energy

Page 189: 1. A, **2.** H, **3.** B, **4.** J, **5.** A, **6.** G, **7.** D, **8.** F

◆ **Lesson 4 Writing Business Letters**

Page 190: 1. July 10, 2004 **2.** 1634 Superior Ave. **3.** Ogden, Utah 84401 **4.** Dear Dr. Lee: **5.** Dear Sir: **6.** Very truly yours,

Page 191: *Heading:* March 15, 2005 *Inside Address:* (line 1) Wisconsin Weekends, Inc. *(line 2)* 300 Shore Rd. *(line 3)* Milwaukee, Wisconsin 53202 *Salutation:* Dear Sir or Madam: *Body:* (first line indented) I am

planning a trip to Milwaukee, Wisconsin, with my family this summer. Please send me information about attractions that might appeal to my daughters, ages five and seven. Thank you in advance for your help. *Closing:* Sincerely yours, *Signature:* Elena Ruiz *Name:* Elena Ruiz

Page 192: Wording of the body of the letter may vary. Heading, inside address, greeting, and closing must be capitalized and punctuated correctly.

Page 193: 1. A, **2.** G, **3.** B, **4.** H, **5.** D

◆ **Unit 6 Assessment**

Pages 195–197: 1. C, **2.** J, **3.** A, **4.** G, **5.** D, **6.** H, **7.** B, **8.** F, **9.** C, **10.** G, **11.** A, **12.** G, **13.** C, **14.** H, **15.** B, **16.** F, **17.** D, **18.** H, **19.** A, **20.** G